ADAPTED GAMES
& ACTIVITIES

FROM TAG
TO TEAM BUILDING

ADAPTED GAMES & ACTIVITIES

FROM TAG
TO TEAM BUILDING

Pattie Rouse

Human Kinetics

Library of Congress Cataloging-in-Publication Data

Rouse, Pattie, 1960-
Adapted games & activities : from tag to team building / Pattie Rouse.
    p. cm.
Includes bibliographical references.
ISBN 0-7360-5432-4 (pbk.)
1. Physical education for children with mental disabilities. 2. Life skills--Study and teaching (Elementary)--Activity programs. 3. Inclusive education. I. Title: Adapted games and activities. II. Title.
GV445.R68 2005
796'.087--dc22
                    2004008299
ISBN-10: 0-7360-5432-4
ISBN-13: 978-0-7360-5432-4

Acquisitions Editor: Bonnie Pettifor; **Developmental Editor:** Jennifer Sekosky; **Assistant Editor:** Ragen E. Sanner/Derek Campbell; **Copyeditor:** Patricia MacDonald; **Proofreader:** Sue Fetters; **Permission Manager:** Dalene Reeder; **Graphic Designer:** Fred Starbird; **Graphic Artist:** Dawn Sills; **Photo Manager:** Kareema McLendon; **Cover Designer:** Andrea Souflee; **Photographer (cover):** Pattie Rouse; **Photographer (interior):** All interior photos by Pattie Rouse except pages 5 and 15 by Kim Thorne; **Art Manager:** Kelly Hendren; **Illustrator:** Argosy; **Printer:** United Graphics

We thank the Cherokee County School District in Georgia for assistance in providing the locations for the photos for this book.

Printed in the United States of America   10 9 8 7 6 5 4 3

Human Kinetics
Website: www.HumanKinetics.com

United States: Human Kinetics
P.O. Box 5076
Champaign, IL 61825-5076
800-747-4457
e-mail: humank@hkusa.com

Canada: Human Kinetics
475 Devonshire Road Unit 100
Windsor, ON N8Y 2L5
800-465-7301 (in Canada only)
e-mail: orders@hkcanada.com

Europe: Human Kinetics
107 Bradford Road
Stanningley
Leeds LS28 6AT, United Kingdom
+44 (0) 113 255 5665
e-mail: hk@hkeurope.com

Australia: Human Kinetics
57A Price Avenue
Lower Mitcham, South Australia 5062
08 8372 0999
e-mail: liaw@hkaustralia.com

New Zealand: Human Kinetics
Division of Sports Distributors NZ Ltd.
P.O. Box 300 226 Albany
North Shore City
Auckland
0064 9 448 1207
e-mail: info@humankinetics.co.nz

This book is dedicated to my students for teaching me how to teach them more effectively, for giving me inspiration each day, and for teaching me the true meaning of joy.

CONTENTS

KEY FOR GAME DIAGRAMS

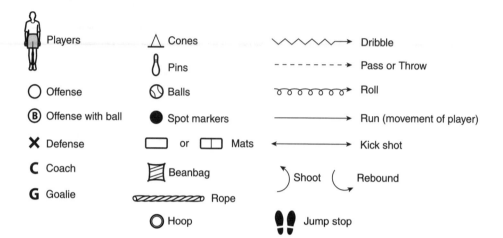

Players	△ Cones	∿∿∿∿→ Dribble
○ Offense	⌘ Pins	– – – – → Pass or Throw
Ⓑ Offense with ball	◐ Balls	⚬⚬⚬⚬⚬→ Roll
✕ Defense	▢ Spot markers	——→ Run (movement of player)
C Coach	▭ or ▭ Mats	←——→ Kick shot
G Goalie	▨ Beanbag	⟩ Shoot ⟨ Rebound
	▱ Rope	
	◎ Hoop	👣 Jump stop

Basketball Court Set-Up

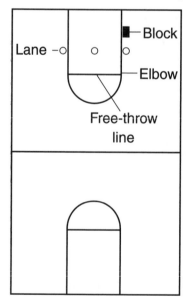

Lane — Block

Elbow

Free-throw line

GAME FINDER

GAME NAME	PLAYERS	SKILLS	EQUIPMENT	PAGE #
30-Second Drill	Small or large group	Shooting	Basketball	131
Balancing Sticks	Any size group	Following directions; directionality; hand–eye coordination	Balancing sticks (3-foot plastic dowels or plastic golf tubes) Spot markers	7
Ball Skills	Any size group	Following directions; directionality; hand–eye coordination	Playground balls or 7- to 8-1/2" bouncing balls Spot markers	9
Balloon Soccer	Small group	Teamwork; kicking; fitness	2 hula hoops 1 balloon Pinnies 4 cones for boundaries	132
Balloon Volley	Small or large group	Cooperation; hand–eye coordination	Balloons	135
Baseball Pin Ball	Small group	Hand–eye coordination; turn taking; aiming; force	Large plastic bat Tee or large cone Sponge ball 4 bowling pins	137
Basketball Shuffle	Small or large group	Passing; shooting; focusing	Playground ball or basketball Goal Music	139

(continued)

GAME NAME	PLAYERS	SKILLS	EQUIPMENT	PAGE #
Beanbag Skills	Any size group	Hand–eye coordination; tossing; catching; following directions	Beanbags Spot markers	11
Bounce and Score	Small or large group	Throwing; agility; tracking; teamwork	4 cones 2 gator-skin balls (coated foam balls) Rope or spot markers for boundary line	59
Box Ball	Small or large group	Agility; throwing; teamwork	Mats or large boxes 10 or more gator-skin balls (coated foam balls) Cones Rope or tape	61
Build a Square	Small group	Trust; teamwork; communication	Rope Blindfolds	63
Bumper Ball	Small or large group	Throwing accuracy	Large therapy ball Beanbags or soft balls Rope or tape for boundary lines	65
Bumper Pool	Small or large group	Rolling accuracy; force; strategy	8-10 lightweight balls Rope or tape for circle boundary 5" playground ball	141

Game	Group size	Skills	Equipment	Page
Capture the Flag	Small or large group	Dodging; fitness; teamwork; strategy	30" or larger cone Object for flag 3 pinnies Tape or spot markers for circle boundary	27
Changing Sides	Small or large group	Following directions; spatial awareness; locomotor skills; creativity	Cones, spot markers, or tape for boundary lines	13
Chicken Tag	Small group	Fitness; following directions	Rubber chicken Spot markers	30
Circle Bowler	Small group	Rolling; aiming; fitness; following rules; turn taking	Spot markers Bowling pin 10" playground ball	143
Circle Dodgeball	Small or large group	Dodging; throwing; catching	1 or 2 8-1/2" gator-skin balls (coated foam balls) Spot markers	32
Circle Pass	Small or large group	Passing; faking; pivoting; defending the pass	Basketball	145
Crocodile Waters	Small group	Teamwork; trust; communication	Scooter board Long rope Plastic bat Tape or rope for boundary lines	67
Double Dribble Basketball	2-5 players per team (2 or more teams)	Teamwork; dribbling; passing; catching	Basketball Pinnies	105

(continued)

GAME FINDER *(continued)*

GAME NAME	PLAYERS	SKILLS	EQUIPMENT	PAGE #
Dribble and Jump Stop Drill	Small or large group	Dribbling; ball handling; stopping with control	Basketballs	147
Dribble, Pass, and Shoot	Any size group	Dribbling; passing; shooting	Soccer balls 2 cones	149
Face-Off	Small group	Agility; hand–eye coordination	8-10 soft balls Tape or rope for circle boundaries 2 bowling pins	107
Flag Tag	Small or large group	Agility; fitness	Flag football flags	34
Follow the Leader	Small group	Giving directions; following directions; communication; trust	1 hula hoop per pair 3 or 4 balls per pair 6-10 bowling pins Blindfolds Tape or spot markers for boundary lines	36
Foot Ball	6-12 players	Communication; teamwork; focusing; problem solving	Balls of various sizes	70
Four Corner Goalie	Any size group	Kicking; blocking	Foam balls or soft balls 8 cones	151

Activity	Group Size	Focus	Equipment	Page
Frisbee Pin Ball	Small group	Throwing accuracy with Frisbees	2 Frisbees per player Rope for circle boundary 10 bowling pins Spot markers or hula hoops	153
Guard the Pin	Small group	Agility; throwing; teamwork	Bowling pin 8-1/2" gator-skin ball (coated foam ball) Rope or spot markers for circle boundary	72
Guard the Square	Small or large group	Throwing; reacting; teamwork	8-1/2" gator-skin ball (coated foam) or sponge ball Rope for circle boundary Tape	74
Help Me Tag	Small or large group	Sharing; communication	Rubber ring, ball, or rubber chicken	39
Hoop Activities	Small or large group	Balance; spatial awareness; following directions	Hula hoops	15
Hotshot Hockey	3-5 players per team (2 or more teams)	Passing and shooting with a hockey stick; teamwork	8 cones Tape or spot markers Pinnies Softball-size Wiffle ball (or foam ball) for the puck Hockey sticks	109
I See	Small or large group	Spatial awareness; body management; fitness	None	18

(continued)

GAME FINDER *(continued)*

GAME NAME	PLAYERS	SKILLS	EQUIPMENT	PAGE #
Jump, Stop, and Shoot	Small or large group	Jump stop; dribbling; shooting	Basketball	155
Layup Drill	Small or large group	Dribbling; layup shooting; passing	Basketballs 2 cones	157
Layup From Pass	Small or large group	Dribbling; passing; layup shooting	Basketballs Spot markers	159
Line Ball	Small group	Striking; catching; teamwork	8-1/2" gator-skin ball (coated foam ball) Tape or rope for boundary lines	76
Locomotor Skills	Any size group	Hopping; skipping; jumping; galloping; walking; running; leaping; sliding	Locomotor flash cards Music	20
Mud Pies	Small or large group	Throwing; teamwork	2 or 3 mats Fleece balls or foam balls	78
Musical Line	Small or large group	Listening; fitness; creativity	Music Tape or spot markers for boundary lines	41
Nod and Go	Small or large group	Communication	Spot markers	80

Activity	Group size	Skills/focus	Equipment	Page
Noodle Balloon Volley	Small or large group	Hand–eye coordination; striking; strategy; teamwork	Balloon Foam noodles (approx. 3 feet long) Pinnies Tape or rope for boundary lines	82
One Square	Small group	Catching; tracking; competing; positive sports behavior	8-1/2" gator-skin ball (coated foam) or 10" playground ball Tape or Velcro for boundary lines	84
One-Base Tee Ball	Any size group	Hand–eye coordination; sequencing; turn taking	Large plastic bat Wiffle ball Tee or large cone Base	161
One-Bounce Volleyball	3-8 players per team (2 teams)	Hand–eye coordination; teamwork	Volleyball net Volleyball 4 cones for boundaries	112
One-on-One Basketball	Small or large group	Defensive skills; offensive skills; transition	Basketball	163
One-on-One Soccer	Any size group	Dribbling under defensive pressure; passing; shooting; defense	2 cones Soccer ball or gator-skin ball (coated foam ball)	165

(continued)

GAME FINDER (continued)

GAME NAME	PLAYERS	SKILLS	EQUIPMENT	PAGE #
Paddle Ball	4-15	Hand–eye coordination; tracking; teamwork	Paddle 12 or more Wiffle balls Crate or basket	167
Partner Beanbag Grab	Any size group	Coordination; listening; following directions	Beanbags	23
Partner Mile Run	Any size group	Fitness; flexibility; agility	Cones to set up the track Fitness cards	114
Partner Rebound	Small or large group	Rebounding; one-on-one skills	Basketball	169
Pickup Dribble	Small or large group	Gaining control in a loose-ball situation; dribbling; shooting	Basketballs	171
Pin Kickball	Small group	Kicking; sequencing; following rules	6-12 bowling pins Playground balls or gator-skin balls (coated foam balls) Spot markers	173
Pop It	Small group	Coordination; fitness; dodging	Yarn Balloons	43
Power Pull	Any size group	Strengthening	Rope 2 spot markers Gloves	175
Rebound and Score	Small or large group	Rebounding; shooting	Basketballs	177

Name	Group size	Skills	Equipment	Page
Ringmaster	Small group	Throwing; dodging; teamwork	8-1/2" gator-skin ball (coated foam) or sponge ball Rope for circle boundary Pinny	86
The River	Small group	Problem solving; teamwork; trust	Blocks of wood Tape or rope for boundary lines	88
Roller Ball	Small or large group	Fitness; dodging	Large therapy ball	45
Rollout Dribble	Any size group	Chasing loose balls; getting control of the ball; dribbling	Soccer balls or gator-skin balls (coated foam balls)	179
Roundball	3-5 players per team (2 or more teams)	Throwing; catching; dribbling; teamwork	2 large cones 2 large playground balls Funnel or small plunger Pinnies 4 cones for boundaries Ball for passing Tape or spot markers	116
Safety Zone Football	6 or more	Throwing; catching; teamwork	Football Pinnies 4 cones for boundaries Spot markers	119
Scatter Tag	Small or large group	Running; dodging	Gator-skin ball (coated foam) or plain foam ball	47

(continued)

GAME FINDER *(continued)*

GAME NAME	PLAYERS	SKILLS	EQUIPMENT	PAGE #
Snowball	8 or more	Throwing; dodging; bending or crouching; following directions	4-6 gator-skin balls (coated foam balls) 4-6 mats Music	49
Soccer Tag	Small or large group	Dribbling; shooting; fitness	4 cones for boundaries 1 or more softer soccer balls	181
Striker Kickball	Small or large group	Striking; hand–eye coordination; teamwork	Bases Lightweight ball or bladder ball	90
Survive for Five	Small group	Throwing; teamwork	Velcro vest with balls Various objects Rope, tape, or spot markers for boundary lines	92
Tag and Drop	Small or large group	Dodging; following directions; fitness	Gator-skin balls (coated foam) or sponge balls	51
Tap and Tag	Small or large group	Striking; catching; dodging; fitness	2 or more 8-1/2" gator-skin balls (coated foam balls) or plain foam balls	53
Target Baseball	Small or large group	Throwing; catching; teamwork	Bases Target Wiffle ball or 8-1/2" gator-skin ball (coated foam ball)	94

Name	Group size	Skills	Equipment	Page
Team Beanbag (Treasure) Grab	Small or large group	Agility; following directions; fitness	Beanbags or various other objects Music Tape or spot markers for boundary lines	96
Team Goalie Score	Small or large group	Dribbling; shooting; passing if desired	2 cones for each goal 4-6 bowling pins for each goal Soccer balls or indoor soccer balls Spot markers	183
Team Handball	4-6 players per team (2 teams)	Teamwork; throwing; catching; dribbling	Playground ball or other high-bouncing ball Pinnies 4 cones for boundaries Tape	122
Three on Three	3 players per team (2 or more teams)	Teamwork; fitness	Soccer ball, hockey sticks, or Pillo Polo set Pinnies 4 cones	124
Treasure Chest	Small group	Teamwork; agility	24 beanbags Rope or spot markers for circle boundary	98
Turkey Hunt	Small group	Fitness	5 or 6 flag football flags	55

(continued)

GAME FINDER *(continued)*

GAME NAME	PLAYERS	SKILLS	EQUIPMENT	PAGE #
Ultimate Frisbee	2-8 players per team (2 or more teams)	Throwing a Frisbee; catching; teamwork	3-5 Frisbees per team Pinnies 4 cones for boundaries Target	126
Volcano Eruption	Small or large group	Throwing; teamwork	3-4 mats 25-50 soft balls Cones	100
Volley Toss	Small group	Underhand tossing; catching	Volleyball net 8-1/2" gator-skin ball (coated foam ball) 4 cones or spot markers for boundaries	185

PREFACE

Imagine a room in which the students do not know intimidation, a space in which all the occupants are nonjudgmental, not caring what the labels on T-shirts or sneakers say. It is the least of their worries whether they are fast or slow; they simply want to participate. Picture a room in which everybody celebrates when they hear "Score!" being yelled excitedly. Emphasis on the winner is irrelevant and unnecessary. Within a classroom that is conducive to the abilities of the students, all of these situations are possible. With the right approach, proper patience, and affective techniques, instructors can totally participate in the joy of teaching unique learners.

Adapted Games and Activities is written for adapted physical education teachers who teach students that are intellectually disabled. Additionally, it is written for the self-contained classroom teacher of these same students as a resource for teacher-directed physical education and for enriching recess activities. This book can also serve as a resource for camp directors or recreational therapists who work with people of all ages with intellectual disabilities. Furthermore, the activities in this book would be appropriate for elementary teachers of regular education in grades K-6.

My hope is that we teach the importance of fun play. Cooperative games provide a fun way to teach fundamental motor and sport skills and concepts and to develop fitness levels. Running does not have to be boring; fleeing, dodging, and chasing are just as beneficial but more exciting. Bending, stretching, jumping jacks, and high jumps (jumping from bent knee position) build strength and endurance. Participating in a nonjudgmental and safe environment builds self-esteem. Being nice to others shows respect and brings feelings of fulfillment in return. Feeling successful gives our children strength.

Games inherently appeal to all children. Nothing better sparks their interest than a new game. I invite you to try these games to help generate excitement and to provide your students with the opportunity to develop their social and motor capabilities.

Motivation is the key to any program. I suggest that you try to motivate with fun. Students who are intellectually disabled often have low motivation to participate because of the lack of opportunities to play and their lower skill levels. Participation in fun games not only provides physical benefits by urging children to move but also offers opportunities for learning how to share, express feelings, set goals, and function independently.

My decision to write this book was influenced by the positive results I've had using games with all groups of learners. I continue to be amazed by the effects of fun play. As a teacher of experiential learning, I use games to develop team-building skills. I've witnessed elementary students acquire a voice and gain personal strength with this voice. I've seen students with behavior problems find peace and calmness and in turn feel wanted and respected by their peers. I've heard teachers express life-altering changes from participating in a one-week training course in the same type of team-building programs. I can attest to young and old alike becoming protective and supportive of others, instead of demeaning, from the sheer joy of play. Students with intellectual disabilities can benefit in much the same way as other learners by playing fun games, and I would like to share some of these activities.

The enthusiasm shown in the delivery of these games will increase the groups' involvement. Focus on positive reinforcement and never hesitate to step in to participate if needed. Realize that it is necessary at times to stop or to slow down for some students. As an educator of this extraordinary genre of children, I know that these children are extremely tolerant and patient.

The games and activities in this book are organized by chapter. Each chapter focuses on a particular type of game, including teacher-directed games, team-building games, and lead-up sport participation games.

An ongoing debate within the field of adapted physical education questions whether to present games and activities to the developmentally disabled student based on developmental age or chronological age. Since you know your students best, the organization by type of game, rather than age or grade level, will allow you to decide which games in this book are appropriate for your students.

Variations for each game are provided, as well as modifications and teaching notes based on how the students respond to each game. The games are simple with few rules, making them easy for the students to comprehend. Furthermore, minimum equipment is needed for the setup of each game or activity, which reduces instructor preparation time.

Chapter 1 introduces the concept that fun play is an excellent tool for teaching motor skills, sport skills, and social skills and developing fitness levels. It also includes a list of strategies useful for delivering the games in this book and for working with developmentally disabled students in general.

Chapter 2 is a short collection of teacher-directed games and activities. These will allow you to work on specific skills and movements with your students while having fun at the same time. They offer an excellent way to develop fine motor skills and lots of opportunity for adaptation and variation.

Tag, chase, and dodge games are the focus of chapter 3. These games are non-eliminating, and often more than one person is needed to be "it." The games are success-oriented, concentrating on leading away from the "failure" aspect. Opportunities for positive reinforcement are provided when emphasis is on participation and not on the score. The interactive nature of these games gives the children a sense of belonging and self-confidence, regardless of their physical abilities.

Chapter 4 consists of team-building and cooperative games and activities aimed at teaching group dynamics, self-esteem, respect, and trust. Most of these activities are problem solving in nature and require guidance from the instructor. The games in this section encourage the importance of respecting others' opinions, along with valuing their ideas. At the end of each activity it is a good idea to hold discussions or debriefings, which allow individuals to give and receive feedback concerning their participation and feelings.

Higher-organization games and activities are located in chapter 5. These games are designed for higher-functioning or older students who need a greater challenge than the low-organization games provide.

Chapter 6 is a collection of lead-up sport and leisure activities. These games will help your students work toward playing sports in a school or community setting or participating in leisure activities. For example, games of Balloon Volley may ultimately lead to development of the skills necessary to play volleyball.

Most of the books written for students with special needs are based on including students in general physical education classes. This book is one of the few written for students with intellectual disabilities that can be taught in a self-contained classroom if that is the least restrictive environment. Furthermore, the activities are appropriate for inclusive situations and appropriate for the use of peer helpers.

A unique feature of this book is that many of the activities include adaptations for learners of all ages and skill levels. Included in the teaching notes is a brief description of how the students respond to the games and other recommendations for using the activities.

Adapted Games and Activities was written to provide fun activities that will enrich any program for students with intellectual disabilities. The games and activities presented here will help your students develop health, social behaviors, fitness and motor skills, and sport and lifetime activity skills. These are some of the most important aspects of inclusion in our society. Learning to communicate in a safe and fun environment is key to their success.

ACKNOWLEDGMENTS

Thanks to my family and friends for being supportive of my endeavors.

Thanks to Denise Palmer for helping me find my strongest voice.

Thanks to Dave Martinez, my APE teaching partner. His knowledge, his computer assistance, and most important his support and willingness to try new things were invaluable.

Thanks to Mary Raley, an incredible administrator, whose passion and professionalism inspired all around her to do their best.

Thanks to all the wonderful teachers that I've met along the way, some who influenced and some who changed my life.

CHAPTER 1

MAKING THE CASE FOR FUN

*A*ll children need a safe environment, physically and emotionally, in order to create a positive attitude toward activity and exercise. When given a choice, people choose activities that they believe to be fun. Fun is often neglected in today's society because we thrive on success and competition. Often students develop a negative attitude about exercise because they are afraid they will fail in the performance of the activity. This results in discontinuance of the activity and possibly in exercise all together.

—Henderson, Glancy, and Little,
Putting the Fun Into Physical Activity

When play for students is based on measurable outcomes, educators often lose sight of the other important aspects of play. The affective components of an activity should also be considered. The activity should promote excitement, spontaneous reactions, caring, confidence, and pride and should be an overall positive personal experience. Physical activity should not be boring or threatening. In addition, it is important to debrief students to help them comprehend these affective social aspects. According to experts, and in accord with my own ideas, educators should remember the importance of fun play, and fun should be the central component of any physical education program.

Most physical educators would agree that games are vehicles for having fun, developing motor skills, and building self-esteem. Simple games that are success oriented motivate students to participate. Games increase students' levels of activity and foster endurance, flexibility, and muscular strength. Students learn to take turns, to be nice, and to cooperate with others. Equally crucial, respect for themselves and others is gained through these experiences. These skills are invaluable for students with intellectual disabilities because of their cognitive, social, and motor delays.

A student with intellectual impairment can play as other children do. One theory is that skills and activities should be appropriate to a student's chronological age and based on activities that same-age peers enjoy. However, a student's functional ability and mental age must also be considered when determining how to present these skills and activities. Modifications and adaptations are clearly needed to reach these objectives for students with intellectual disabilities. Because personal acceptance and the development of proper social relationships are critical to independence, games that promote teamwork, strategy, and fitness can be beneficial to students with intellectual disabilities. Teachers strive to lead their students toward participation in lifetime sport and leisure activities. I believe fun games can initiate and support this process.

Choosing activities for students with severe or profound intellectual disabilities can be a challenge. I have found it helpful to use fun games periodically. Though the comprehension level of these children is usually very low, they appear to enjoy the social stimulation. With the help of teachers' assistants or children without disabilities, students with severe intellectual disabilities can be included in many fun activities. When appropriate, I have provided suggestions and modifications to the activities in this book to make this integration easier and more effective.

Planning activities for students with moderate intellectual disabilities has proven to be an easier task for me in my adapted physical education program. These students are receptive to a broad range of activities. In my experience, they show no resistance to fun games that many would consider appropriate for typical elementary students. They love drills that develop fundamentals for competitive sports such as basketball, hockey, tennis, soccer, and football. With simple modification and social and motor development, students with moderate intellectual disabilities are also successful in modified team sports.

Adapted activities are often successfully used to mainstream students or individuals with mild intellectual disabilities into general physical education. Many of these students or young adults do not have noticeable disabilities but have low social skills from lack of self-worth and lack of opportunities to interact with others. Activities should focus on teamwork, problem solving, and individual challenges. Cooperative learning activities promote a better sense of self-worth and less self-consciousness as well as foster a sense of belonging and increased feelings of acceptance. Low levels of competition will elevate self-esteem if taught in a safe environment developed from team-building activities. Each day should include discussions or debriefings on working together. Lessons should encourage the importance of respecting others' abilities and opinions, along with valuing their ideas. Professionals recognize this type of learning to be an important teaching component for all children, with or without disabilities.

Often, children with intellectual disabilities are unable to absorb or comprehend information at the same rate as children without disabilities; therefore adaptations are needed. I have found the following strategies useful for delivering the games in this book:

- ⊙ Use a consistent routine: warm-up, activity or game, closing.
- ⊙ Expect students to participate, expect them to be nice to others, and expect them to listen when you are talking.

- ⊙ Give lots of specific praise.
- ⊙ Use concrete boundaries: lines, ropes, and cones. Use pinnies to distinguish "it" or opposite teams. Use spot markers for students having difficulty staying on task.
- ⊙ Modify equipment by using nonintimidating balls for tag games and using lighter balls and rackets.
- ⊙ Modify for different learners' needs before and during activities. Inform the learners of these modifications if necessary.
- ⊙ Give easy and precise directions followed by a demonstration of the skill or rule.
- ⊙ Teach in the moment (be flexible). Plan extra activities as a backup for each lesson.
- ⊙ Celebrate the process, not just the product. Be careful with the criticism.
- ⊙ Allow varying levels of participation. Eventually these levels increase with an individual's feeling of comfort.

When activities are taught to meet the students' needs, the activities become more fun because the risk of failure is minimized. All activities should challenge the students; however, it is important to keep the success rate high. This philosophy supports the need to modify or individualize activities to meet the levels of unique learners. The most important gift to students with intellectual disabilities is praise, praise, and more praise. Positive reinforcement does more for self-esteem than mastering any physical skill. Smiles, high fives, and cheers definitely seem to motivate and stimulate my students. If their enthusiasm is any indication, the development of this book has been a success. I have seen remarkable change in the students' attitudes toward participation, and it is my experience that having fun increases their self-esteem. We laugh a lot and we play hard. In essence, we have *fun!*

CHAPTER 2

FOLLOW ME

Teacher-Directed Games and Activities

Younger students, both with and without intellectual disabilities, need to learn movement concepts and practice skills before they can successfully participate in organized games. The activities in this chapter integrate movement concepts and skills. The students manipulate equipment and practice spatial and body awareness in an organized learning environment.

You are the director, giving both verbal and visual cues to demonstrate each skill. The activities require that each student have his or her own personal equipment, which reinforces self-control and proper use of equipment. Be prepared to monitor closely during this stage of acquisition. You must emphasize safety rules and ensure that students abide by them to avoid incidents and ensure skill development. Music can be a great motivational tool to use during the class to practice learned skills.

These developmental skill activities can serve as a prerequisite for elementary students to advance to more organized team games. It is recommended to close with an activity such as Scatter Tag or Roller Ball (see chapter 3) to provide fitness and fun.

━━━ BALANCING STICKS ━━━

Players

Any size group

Area

Gym, multipurpose room, or outdoor open area

Skills

Following directions • directionality • hand–eye coordination

Equipment

Balancing stick for each student (3-foot plastic dowels or plastic golf tubes) • spot markers

Activity

1. Students should be scattered in personal spaces. Using spot markers will help them stay in their personal spaces.
2. Instruct the students that "Freeze" means to stop and hold the stick in one hand.
3. This activity is teacher directed with verbal cues and teacher demonstration.
4. Remind the students of safety rules (equipment can't be used as swords or bats and can't be thrown in the air).

Teacher's Verbal Cues

Show me how you can do the following:

- Balance the stick on the palms of both hands.
- Balance the stick on the back of both hands.
- Balance the stick on both feet.
- Hold the stick on the top with one finger while the bottom of the stick is touching the ground, then walk around the stick.
- Still holding the stick with one finger, let go and catch the stick before it hits the ground.
- Hold the stick out in front of your body with a hand on each end. Step over the stick as you still hold it.

- ◎ Hold the stick with one finger. Let go, spin around, and catch the stick before it hits the ground.
- ◎ Hold the stick in the middle with one hand. Let go and catch it with the other hand.
- ◎ Make a letter with the stick on the ground using your body.
- ◎ Make a number with the stick on the ground using your body.
- ◎ Balance the stick with one finger on the end of the stick.
- ◎ Balance the stick with the palm of your hand.

Variations

Make it easier:

Demonstrate each skill with students in sitting "freeze" position, then allow them to try the skill.

Make it more difficult:

Have the students follow directions using only verbal cues instead of demonstration of the skill.

Adaptations

- ◎ For balancing stunts, use peer helpers or teacher assistants for students in wheelchairs and for students who are blind or visually impaired.
- ◎ Give personal directions to students with autism or to students who do not seem to comprehend.

Teaching Notes

The students need constant feedback and monitoring in respect to safety.

=== BALL SKILLS ===

Players

Any size group

Area

Gym or outdoor open area

Skills

Following directions • directionality • hand–eye coordination

Equipment

Playground balls or 7- to 8-1/2-inch bouncing balls • spot markers

Activity

1. Students should be scattered in personal spaces. Using spot markers will help them stay in their personal spaces.
2. Instruct the students that "Freeze" means to stop and show the ball to you.
3. Stress keeping their eyes on the ball at all times.
4. This activity is teacher directed with verbal cues and teacher demonstration.
5. Demonstrate high, medium, and low levels.
6. Start in a sitting position.

Teacher's Verbal Cues

Show me how you can do the following:

- Toss the ball and catch it with both hands.
- Toss the ball at a low level from hand to hand.
- Roll the ball back and forth from hand to hand in front of your body.
- Roll the ball around your body.
- Stand up. Drop the ball and catch it.
- Toss the ball up and catch it.
- Toss the ball up, let it bounce, and then catch it.

⊙ Push the ball with one hand and catch it. (Dribble once.)

⊙ Push the ball with both hands and catch it.

⊙ Stand next to the wall. Roll the ball against the wall and then catch it.

⊙ Bounce the ball against the wall and then catch it.

Variations

Make it easier:

⊙ For small or less skilled groups, you may choose to toss and roll the ball to each student individually.

⊙ Use only a few of the listed skills, and add others on another day.

Make it more difficult:

Make the students perform the skills with a partner.

Adaptations

⊙ Keep verbal cues and teacher demonstration separate by giving verbal cues first and then demonstrating the skills for the students.

⊙ Use peer helpers or teacher assistants for any students who are unable to toss or catch the ball.

Teaching Notes

⊙ Allow creative playtime either before or after the activity time. Allow students to roll or toss the balls with a partner. Or students can play with the balls using any or all of the skills that they choose from the earlier activities.

⊙ Use music during the creative playtime.

━━ BEANBAG SKILLS ━━

Players

Any size group

Area

Gymnasium, classroom, or open area, indoors or out

Skills

Hand–eye coordination • tossing • catching • following directions

Equipment

Beanbag for each student • spot markers

Activity

1. Students should be scattered in personal spaces. Using spot markers will help them stay in their personal spaces.
2. Instruct the students that "freeze" means to stop and show the beanbag to you.
3. Stress keeping their eyes on the beanbag at all times.
4. This activity is teacher directed with verbal cues and teacher demonstration.
5. Demonstrate high, medium, and low levels.
6. Divide the students into partners, and tell them to practice any skills performed during class.

Teacher's Verbal Cues

Show me how you can do the following:

⊙ Toss and catch with both hands. (Allow three to five tosses.)
⊙ Toss with one hand and catch with the other hand.
⊙ Toss with one hand and catch with that same hand.
⊙ Toss with the other hand and catch with that hand.
⊙ Toss the beanbag at a medium level and catch it at a low level.
⊙ Toss the beanbag and catch it above your head.
⊙ Balance the beanbag on your shoulder.

◎ Balance the beanbag on your back, then knee, then foot.

◎ Place the beanbag on the back of your hand. Toss it and catch it.

◎ Toss the beanbag, clap, and then catch it.

◎ Toss the beanbag, spin around, and then catch it.

Variations

Make it easier:

Use fleece balls or sponge balls.

Make it more difficult:

◎ Add more advanced skills for more advanced groups.

◎ Start in a sitting position and end up in a standing position.

Adaptations

◎ Use peer helpers or teacher assistants for students in wheelchairs and for students who are blind or visually impaired.

◎ Use hand over hand when necessary, or use Velcro balls and gloves.

Teaching Notes

◎ You probably will not use all of these activities the first time you do this skill work. It is very difficult for the students to stay focused and in a personal space for long periods.

◎ Use background music during creative playtime.

◎ Finish this activity with a fast-paced game such as Scatter Tag (see chapter 3).

━━━ CHANGING SIDES ━━━

Players

Small or large group

Area

Gym or open area, indoors or out

Skills

Following directions • spatial awareness • locomotor skills • creativity

Equipment

Cones, spot markers, or tape for boundary lines

Activity

1. Set up two parallel boundary lines approximately 20 to 25 feet apart. If you're using the gym, the sidelines are perfect.
2. Teach the students a silent signal for changing sides (e.g., when you touch your elbow, knee, or nose).
3. Before you give the "go" signal, discuss the manner in which the students will change to the other side (e.g., hop, skip, jump, gallop, leap, slide, walk, bear walk, duck walk, as a plane).
4. Stress to the students that they cannot touch others.
5. When students get to the opposite side, they sit on the line.
6. At your request, they may give the person on each side of them a high five.

Variations

Make it easier:

⊙ Shorten the distance between boundary lines.

⊙ Allow all students to change as one group from side to side.

Make it more difficult:

Start the game with players on each sideline, with the objective being to see which team can be the first sitting on the line after changing sides.

Adaptations

- ⊙ Push students in wheelchairs if they are not mobile.
- ⊙ Lead students who are blind or visually impaired with a tether.
- ⊙ Give direct verbal signals to those who need it.

Teaching Notes

- ⊙ This activity is good for students who have a difficult time staying focused.
- ⊙ Students must watch for the "go" signal instead of hearing it.

━━━ HOOP ACTIVITIES ━━━

Players

Small or large group

Area

Gym or open area, indoors or out

Skills

Balance • spatial awareness • following directions

Equipment

Hula hoop for each student

Activity

1. Students should be scattered in personal spaces, and each student has a hula hoop.
2. This activity is teacher directed with verbal cues and teacher demonstration.
3. It is recommended to allow the students to try the hula hoop before attempting structured skills.
4. You must demonstrate this skill for the students.
5. Next, instruct the students to sit inside their hoops, then begin the skills.

Teacher's Verbal Cues

Show me how you can do the following:

- Sit on your bottom and lift your feet in the air.
- Grab your toes while your feet are still in the air.
- Make the number one with your body inside your hoop.
- Stand on one foot and keep your balance. Stand on the other foot.
- Jump at a low level, then a medium level with little force.
- Jump from one side of the hoop to the other.
- Stand outside your hoop. Hop around your hoop on one foot.
- Make a number with your hoop and your body.
- Practice hula hooping in your personal space.

Variations

Make it easier:

Use fewer cues for groups with attention deficit problems.

Make it more difficult:

- Use ropes instead of hoops, and add skills such as walking on the rope or jumping over the rope while on the ground.
- Add more skills for advanced groups.
- Allow students to create their own tricks and share them with the class.

Adaptations

- ⊙ Allow students in wheelchairs to get out of their chairs if possible or use walkers if any of these students have one available.
- ⊙ Some students may need a spot marker to help them stay in a personal space, especially students with autism who need more concrete boundaries.

Teaching Notes

- ⊙ Ropes and hoops are interchangeable for most of these skills.
- ⊙ The students will need a lot of assistance when attempting to hula hoop or jump rope.
- ⊙ Play a game for your closing activity or use music for creative playtime.

Players

Small or large group

Area

Gym or open area, indoors or out

Skills

Spatial awareness • body management • fitness

Equipment

None

Activity

1. Discuss the direction that the kids will be moving about (counterclockwise, or the same direction as at the skating rink).

2. You will say, "I see . . ." and the students will respond with, "What do you see?" Your response is what the students pretend to be.

Teacher's Verbal Cues

Show me how you can be the following:

- I see horses galloping through the pastures.
- I see snakes slithering through the grass.
- I see planes flying high in the sky.
- I see sharks swimming in the ocean.
- I see bees buzzing around.
- I see soldiers marching in a parade.
- I see bears in the forest.
- I see raindrops falling from the sky.
- I see racecars racing around the track.
- I see monkeys swinging through the trees.
- I see ducks swimming in the lake.

Variations

Make it easier:

Use easier "I See" verbal cues such as: trees moving their leaves in the wind or elephants walking and lifting their trunks.

Make it more difficult:

Use more difficult "I See" verbal cues such as: kids leaping over a river or a frog hopping.

Adaptations

Use peer helpers or teacher assistants for students in wheelchairs and for students who are blind or visually impaired.

Teaching Notes

This is a good game for teaching elementary students to follow directions and for developing or increasing fitness levels.

Adapted from R. Bryant and E. Oliver, 1974, *Complete elementary physical education guide* (West Nyack, NY: Parker).

--- LOCOMOTOR SKILLS ---

Players

Any size group

Area

Gym

Skills

Hopping • skipping • jumping • galloping • walking • running •
leaping • sliding

Equipment

Locomotor flash cards • music

Activity

1. Make locomotor flash cards with the skills written on the front. The cards should be large enough for the students to read from a distance (8 inches by 15 inches).
2. Demonstrate the skills to the students:
   - ⊙ Hopping—hop on one foot, then the other
   - ⊙ Skipping—step and a hop, changing feet
   - ⊙ Jumping—jump on two feet
   - ⊙ Galloping—forward step and a hop
   - ⊙ Walking—step and alternate feet
   - ⊙ Running—fast walk
   - ⊙ Leaping—run and jump, stretching the front leg out
   - ⊙ Sliding—sideways step and a hop
3. Teach the students to move in the same direction (counterclockwise, or the same direction as at the skating rink).
4. Choose motivating music. I find the "Freeze" song from the CD by "Steve & Greg" very appropriate because it also teaches the students to freeze.
5. Remind the students to keep their "bumpers up" (arms up and bent at the elbows when approaching other players).

Variations

Make it easier:

- ⊙ Use as a warm-up with songs that have a slower beat.
- ⊙ Use as an opening or closing activity.
- ⊙ Allow the students to travel from side to side of the gym instead of in a circular motion.

Make it more difficult:

Use as a fitness activity and play several songs.

Adaptations

⊙ Use peer helpers or teacher assistants for students in wheel-chairs and for students who are blind or visually impaired.

⊙ Perform the skills with the students to motivate the students or to model the preferred skills.

Teaching Notes

This is a great fitness activity and can also be a great closing activity.

--- PARTNER BEANBAG GRAB ---

Players

Any size group (divided into partners)

Area

Classroom or open area, indoors or out

Skills

Coordination • listening • following directions

Equipment

Beanbag for each group of partners

Activity

1. Start with students sitting on the floor in a cross-legged position facing a partner.
2. A beanbag should be on the floor between each set of partners.
3. This activity is teacher directed with verbal cues and teacher demonstration.
4. Direct the students to place a hand or both hands in a certain position.
5. When you give the "go" signal, the students try to be the first person to grab the beanbag.

Teacher's Verbal Cues

- ⊙ Place your hands on your head.
- ⊙ Place your hands on your knees.
- ⊙ Place your hands on your shoulders.
- ⊙ Place your hands on the floor beside you.
- ⊙ Place one hand on your head and one hand on your belly.
- ⊙ Place your hands together in front of you.
- ⊙ Hold your hands above your head.
- ⊙ Cross your arms across your chest.
- ⊙ Place your hands behind you.
- ⊙ Cover your eyes with your hands.

Variations

Make it easier:

⊙ Place a beanbag for each student on the floor.

⊙ Use the same teacher verbal cue several times in succession.

Make it more difficult:

Make the students sit with their legs in a V position.

Adaptations

⊙ Use a desk between students in wheelchairs.

⊙ Use a beeping ball for students who are blind or visually impaired.

Teaching Notes

⊙ This is a great closing activity.

⊙ The students love it and do not usually turn it into a competition.

⊙ When using this as the main activity, the students enjoy tossing the beanbags with a partner afterward.

YOU'RE IT!

Tag, Chase, and Dodge Games and Activities

Chapter 3 is a compilation of low-organization games designed to promote fun and fitness. The games give the players opportunities to learn the application of rules and regulations. These low-organization games focus on learning to play, learning to share, social skills, cooperation, having fun in a group, and being part of a team. For the most part, the games are non-elimination with little or no emphasis on winning and are continuous in play.

You'll need to teach a few safety concepts before allowing the students to participate. For example, in most tag games it is crucial to teach all players to move in a counterclockwise direction. I tell my students to run in the same direction that they would go if they were skating at the skating rink. Next, I teach my students to put their "bumpers up" when approaching other players. I demonstrate, arms up and bent at the elbows. Additionally, before giving the "go" signal, I instruct my students to start with a fast walk. As the students begin to feel safe and comfortable, they gradually start running on their own.

When you first teach these games, the games themselves will be the main focus of your lesson plan or allotted time period. Once the students become familiar with some of the games, such as Scatter Tag, Tag and Drop, or Tap and Tag, they work well as closing activities for more advanced or organized games.

Games that are suitable for students with severe intellectual disabilities will include modifications to make the games easier. Teacher assistants and peer helpers may be necessary to help these students play the recommended games.

CAPTURE THE FLAG

Players

Small or large group

Area

Gym or open area, indoor or out

Skills

Dodging • fitness • teamwork • strategy

Equipment

30-inch or larger cone • object for flag • 3 pinnies • tape or spot markers for circle boundary (Do not use rope because of the tripping hazard to the players.)

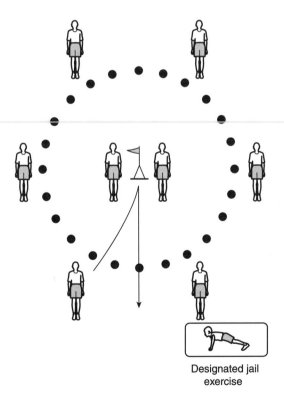

Designated jail
exercise

Activity

1. Form a circle approximately 30 feet in diameter with tape or spot markers.
2. Place a tall cone with a shirt or rag hanging over it in the center of the circle.
3. Set up an area as the designated jail away from the circle boundary.
4. Assign two or three players wearing pinnies to guard the flag in the middle.
5. All other players stand outside the circle boundary.
6. Players on the outside of the circle will try to rush into the circle and take the flag without being tagged.
7. If a player grabs the flag, he or she must carry the flag outside the circle without being tagged to complete the capture or score.
8. When tagged by a guard, players must go to the jail and perform a predetermined exercise before returning to play.
9. Allow guards to protect the flag for two or three minutes before changing guards.
10. If a player captures the flag, reset and give a "go" signal to restart.

Variations

Make it easier:

- Adjust the number of guards according to group size and ability.
- Do not have a designated jail. Students perform exercises outside of the circle boundary.

Make it more difficult:

Make the circle larger.

Adaptations

- Allow children in wheelchairs to crawl if possible or stay in the chairs if the students are mobile.

- Students in wheelchairs only have to grab the flag; they do not need to carry it out of the circle.
- Lead students who are blind or visually impaired with a tether; they only have to grab the flag.

Teaching Notes

- Guarding is the most difficult skill in this game. Choose more skilled guards to help the less skilled or slower students.
- Playing the game a couple of days consecutively will help students understand the game.
- Using a designated jail area is a great idea because the students can do exercises such as sit-ups that require more space than other quick exercises used in tag games.
- Use of rope for creating the circle boundary is not recommended because the circle is easily broken. It also presents a tripping hazard to the players.

━━━ CHICKEN TAG ━━━

Players

Small group

Area

Gym or open area, indoors or out

Skills

Fitness • following directions

Equipment

Rubber chicken • spot markers

Activity

1. Form a circle with spot markers.
2. Instruct the students to stand on a spot marker and hold their hands behind their backs.
3. Choose one student to be "it" and ask him or her to stand outside the circle of players.
4. "It" walks around the circle and eventually places the chicken in another player's hands.
5. "It" runs around the outside of the circle, attempting to get back to the player's open spot before the new player with the chicken tags him or her.
6. If tagged, "it" does two jumping jacks (or other predetermined exercise) and then returns to the open spot.
7. The new "it" continues the game in the same manner.

Variations

Make it easier:

Allow students to walk for all tasks in the activity.

Make it more difficult:

Use other locomotor skills for traveling around the circle such as skipping or galloping.

Adaptations

- ⊙ Push students in wheelchairs if they are not mobile.
- ⊙ Lead students who are blind or visually impaired and students who do not understand the game.

Teaching Notes

When playing this game with younger students or students with more severe intellectual disabilities, it may be necessary to use assistants if the learners' comprehension levels are low. This does not take away the fun of the game. Consider also using another variation, Chicken Toss, in which the student with the chicken calls another student's name and then passes the chicken to that student; this continues until everyone has caught the chicken. This is a good closing activity for working on the skill of instigating conversation.

---CIRCLE DODGEBALL ---

Players

Small or large group

Area

Gym or open area, indoors or out

Skills

Dodging • throwing • catching

Equipment

1 or 2 8-1/2-inch gator-skin balls • spot markers

Activity

1. Form a circle with spot markers, and tell all players to stand on a spot.
2. Instruct two to four students, according to the group size, to stand inside the circle boundary.

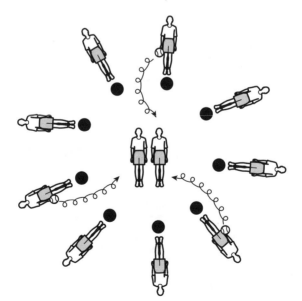

3. When you give the "go" signal, the players standing on the spot markers will roll the ball or balls at the players inside the circle, attempting to tag them on the feet or ankles.

4. When a player is tagged below the waist three times, he or she joins the boundary circle.

5. Once all students have been eliminated from the circle, choose new players to enter the circle.

Variations

Make it easier:

◎ The players in the middle can be a team, and the team exits after five team hits.

◎ Allow one player at a time in the middle when playing this game with elementary students, and help this student avoid the ball. Never force a student to go inside the middle if he or she has reservations.

Make it more difficult:

◎ Use two balls if players are physically advanced.

◎ Have students toss the ball rather than rolling it to tag the players. Students must tag the players inside the circle below the waist.

Adaptations

◎ Assist students who are blind or visually impaired.

◎ For students in wheelchairs, the ball must bounce and may tag the students only on the feet or the back wheel of the chair.

Teaching Notes

◎ Some students are afraid of being hit and want the teacher or a teacher assistant to stand with them inside the circle. Sometimes just showing them the softness of the ball eliminates the fear. I do not force any student to take a turn in the middle.

◎ For the most part, kids love to play dodgeball. My high school students ask to play this game often.

▬▬▬ FLAG TAG ▬▬▬

Players

Small or large group

Area

Gym or open area, indoors or out

Skills

Agility • fitness

Equipment

Flag football flags

Activity

1. Each student is given three or four flags, which are placed in their back pockets or the waistband of their pants.
2. Students will try to pull other students' flags as well as try to avoid others from pulling their flags.
3. The game ends when all flags have been pulled from all students.

Variations

Make it easier:

Allow only walking when the area is small or the group is large.

Make it more difficult:

⊙ Add a task such as picking up objects that are spread around the playing area and placing the objects in a basket.

⊙ A point can be earned for each flag a player pulls.

Adaptations

- ⊙ Push students in wheelchairs if they are not mobile.
- ⊙ Peer helpers or teacher assistants can help pull flags for students in wheelchairs or students who are blind or visually impaired.

Teaching Notes

- ⊙ This is a great fitness activity, especially if you use a lot of flags.
- ⊙ Many of the students will want to give you the flags as soon as they pull them from other players. Encourage the students to hold on to the flags to avoid collisions when approaching you.

=== FOLLOW THE LEADER ===

Players

Small group

Area

Gym or open area, indoors or out

Skills

Giving directions • following directions • communication • trust

Equipment

Hula hoop for each group of partners • 3 or 4 balls inside each hoop • 6 to 10 bowling pins • blindfolds • tape or spot markers for boundary lines

Activity

1. Set up two parallel boundary lines approximately 10 feet apart.

2. Set up the bowling pins on one of the boundary lines; the pins should be approximately 3 feet apart. Students will stand behind the other boundary line and roll the balls toward the pins.

3. Scatter the hula hoops about the area, approximately 15 to 20 feet behind the rolling boundary line.

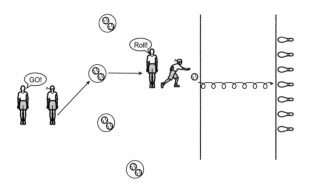

4. Divide the students into partners by likenesses or differences (e.g., height, age, wearing same colors, boys, girls).

5. Instruct the students that one partner will be wearing a blindfold and will be the student rolling the ball.

6. The other partner will guide the student who is blindfolded.

7. The leader's responsibility is to safely guide the blindfolded partner to one of the hoops containing the balls, then to the rolling boundary line, and then follow up with instructions to roll the ball at the pins.

8. The leader will continue until all pins are down or all balls in the hoops have been used.

9. The blindfolded player may pick up only one ball at a time, and all partners will be working at the same time.

10. Instruct the partners to switch positions. Reset the area and continue play until all pins are down or all the balls have been used.

11. Combine the number of pins knocked down by the partners as a team score.

Variations

Make it easier:

⊙ Use two leaders for one blindfolded student.

⊙ Allow the partner to lead the blindfolded partner with a physical touch on the elbow.

Make it more difficult:

Set up the boundary lines a wider distance apart.

Adaptations

Use peer helpers or teacher assistants to push students in wheelchairs or to help them pick up balls.

Teaching Notes

- ⊙ Before starting, discuss directional terms such as stop, go, left, and right.
- ⊙ Stress the importance of being specific for the purpose of safety precautions.
- ⊙ Before the partners switch roles, provide time for them to discuss anything they feel the other needs to know about leading or following.
- ⊙ Be aware that some students find the responsibility of being the leader difficult. After the activity, ask each partner to give positive feedback concerning the other partner's leadership skills.
- ⊙ Discuss how it felt to be blindfolded.
- ⊙ This game is recommended for students with mild intellectual disabilities.

▬▬▬ HELP ME TAG ▬▬▬

Players

Small or large group

Area

Gym or open area

Skills

Sharing • communication

Equipment

Rubber ring, ball, or rubber chicken

Activity

1. This is a tag game in which the students are encouraged to help each other.
2. One person is chosen to be "it," and all other students flee from "it" in walking mode.
3. One player will start with the "helper" object (the rubber ring, ball, or rubber chicken) and is allowed to pass the object to anyone who calls out, "Help me."
4. As long as a player holds the helper object, he or she cannot be tagged by the "it" player.
5. If a player is tagged, he or she does a predetermined exercise before returning to play.
6. When using one helper object, the "it" player should toss it to another player before continuing play.

Variations

Make it easier:

Use several helper objects, and the "it" player can choose to keep an intercepted object or toss it to another player.

Make it more difficult:

Play the game in silence. Ask the students to create a replacement for the verbal "help me."

Adaptations

⊙ Push students in wheelchairs if they are not mobile.

⊙ Lead students who are blind or visually impaired with a tether.

Teaching Notes

⊙ Spend time reflecting on the game:

  • How did it feel to help others?

  • How did it feel to receive help?

⊙ This game is recommended for students with mild intellectual disabilities.

Adapted from a Project Adventure Inc. workshop

---MUSICAL LINE---

Players

Small or large group

Area

Gym or open area, indoors or out

Skills

Listening • fitness • creativity

Equipment

Music • tape or spot markers for boundary lines

Activity

1. Set up two parallel boundary lines approximately 20 to 25 feet apart.
2. Designate one player to stand in the middle as the "it" player.
3. All other players start the game standing on one of the parallel boundaries.
4. When the music starts, the players cross from side to side.
5. Tell the players that they can dance, walk, or move in a creative way when crossing.
6. When the music stops, players attempt to return to either boundary line before being tagged by "it."
7. When tagged, a player does a predetermined exercise before returning to play.
8. Stop and start the music at varying intervals (10-30 seconds).
9. After several stops, choose another "it."

Variations

Make it easier:

Start all students on one line for groups of students with severe intellectual disabilities, and help them cross from side to side. The objective of the game would then become getting to the other side before the music stops. The "it" player would also need assistance.

Make it more difficult:

⊙ Change the tempo of the music.

⊙ Use locomotor skills for crossing (e.g., running, skipping, sliding, or galloping).

⊙ Use an extra "it" player to make it more difficult for the players trying to cross.

Adaptations

⊙ Push students in wheelchairs if they are not mobile.

⊙ Lead students who are blind or visually impaired with a tether.

Teaching Notes

⊙ Students are surprisingly uninhibited when playing this game.

⊙ In my experience, fifth and sixth grade students with mild intellectual disabilities found this game the most fun.

⊙ When playing this game with a large group, the gym sideline boundaries are recommended.

=== POP IT ===

Players

Small group

Area

Gym or open area, indoors or out

Skills

Coordination • fitness • dodging

Equipment

Yarn • balloon for each student

Activity

1. Using the yarn, tie a balloon loosely around the ankle of each player.
2. Instruct the players to scatter around the playing area.
3. When you give the "go" signal, players will start chasing others, attempting to pop the balloons by stepping on them.
4. Players will also try to avoid other players who are attempting to pop their balloons.
5. When a player's balloon is popped, that player continues to participate by attempting to pop other players' balloons.

Variations

Make it easier:

Provide an area for the players to run through, and you are the only one attempting to pop each player's balloon.

Make it more difficult:

Tie a balloon on both ankles of each player.

Adaptations

- Push students in wheelchairs if they are not mobile.
- Lead students who are blind or visually impaired with a tether.
- Inflate extra balloons and help these same students stamp the balloons.

Teaching Notes

- Fun! However, some students may be afraid of the popping balloons, so be sensitive to this situation. Another separate activity may need to be prepared for those particular students.
- This game works well with all levels of learners.

=== ROLLER BALL ===

Stay in Stance

Players

Small or large group

Area

Gym or open area, indoors or out

Skills

Fitness • dodging

Equipment

Large therapy ball

Activity

1. Students should be scattered around the playing area.
2. When you give the "go" signal, one student starts rolling the large ball around, trying to tag other students.
3. When tagged, students must perform a predetermined exercise before returning to play.

Variations

Make it easier:

For younger students, you can act as "it."

Make it more difficult:

Use two large balls for large groups.

Adaptations

◎ Push students in wheelchairs if they are not mobile.
◎ Lead students who are blind or visually impaired with a tether.

Teaching Notes

◎ You, the teacher, need to be "it" when playing this game with elementary students because they can easily be knocked over if "it" is not careful.
◎ This activity can serve as a closing activity once the students have played it a few times.

--- SCATTER TAG ---

Players

Small or large group

Area

Gym or open area

Skills

Running • dodging

Equipment

Gator-skin ball or foam ball

Activity

1. Gather all players to the middle of the playing area. Stand in the center of the group, holding the ball.
2. When you bounce the ball above head level, all players scatter and the chase begins.
3. Chase the players around the playing area.
4. When tagging players, simply say, "Tag."
5. Tagged players then continue to run about.
6. Stop play every minute or two and regroup in the middle to allow rest time.
7. Restart with a bounce of the ball.

Variations

Make it easier:

Allow and assist a student to be "it" when playing with younger students.

Make it more difficult:

⊙ With older students, allow a student to be "it."
⊙ Make tagged players perform a predetermined exercise such as two jumping jacks, high jumps (jumping from bent knee position), toe touches, and the like before returning to play.

Adaptations

⊙ Push students in wheelchairs if they are not mobile.

⊙ Lead students who are blind or visually impaired with a tether.

Teaching Notes

⊙ Initially, it is important to teach the students to run in a counter-clockwise direction.

⊙ This game works well with all groups of learners. Once the students get used to this game, it becomes a great closing activity.

=== SNOWBALL ===

Players

8 or more

Area

Gym or open area

Skills

Throwing • dodging • bending or crouching • following directions

Equipment

4 to 6 gator-skin balls • 4 to 6 mats • music

Activity

1. Arrange the mats in a circular shape around the playing area.
2. Fold the mats so that they are only 2 to 3 feet in height. This ensures that the players will have to get low to the ground and use more leg muscles.
3. Choose two players (both are "it") to stand in the center area of the mats with the balls (snowballs).
4. When the music starts, all other students walk quickly around the mats.

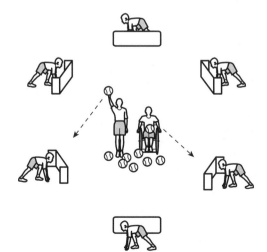

5. When the music stops, the students attempt to hide behind the mats to avoid being tagged by a thrown snowball from the "it" players.

6. If tagged by a snowball, that student must perform a designated exercise before reentering the game.

Variations

Make it easier:

Retrieve balls for the "it" players.

Make it more difficult:

⊙ Use other means of movement around the mats such as skipping, galloping, or running.

⊙ For larger groups, allow more players to be "it."

⊙ Unfold the mats to a taller height, especially if you allow students to run.

Adaptations

⊙ Balls should be rolled at students in wheelchairs and must tag only a back wheel.

⊙ Lead students who are blind or visually impaired with a tether.

⊙ Retrieve balls for "it" players who are visually impaired or in a wheelchair.

Teaching Notes

⊙ This game is a great fitness activity, and the students may need a break between games.

⊙ The students enjoy the risk-taking aspect of this game.

=== TAG AND DROP ===

Players

Small or large group

Area

Gym or open area, indoors or out

Skills

Dodging • following directions • fitness

Equipment

Gator-skin balls or sponge balls

Activity

1. This is a non-elimination tag game in which there is no running. Students are allowed to walk fast.
2. Spread the students out in the playing area, and choose one or two students to be "it."
3. "It" players will have a ball in their hands and will try to tag others with the ball.
4. "It" drops the ball and is no longer "it" when he or she tags another player.
5. At this point, anyone can pick up the ball and become the new "it."
6. The person who was tagged must do two jumping jacks (or other exercise) before continuing the game.

Variations

Make it easier:

- ⊙ If the group is small (4-9), use one "it."
- ⊙ If the group is larger (10-20), use more "its."

Make it more difficult:

Allow the "it" players to tag more than one player (3-5) before dropping the ball.

Adaptations

⊙ Push students in wheelchairs if they are not mobile.

⊙ Lead students who are blind or visually impaired with a tether.

⊙ Allow students in wheelchairs to use only their arms for jumping jacks.

⊙ Allow students in wheelchairs to spin around instead of doing jumping jacks.

Teaching Notes

⊙ It takes some time for the students to get used to the tag and drop, so be ready to remind them a few times.

⊙ Once the students learn this game, it can be a quick closing activity.

=== TAP AND TAG ===

Players

Small or large group

Area

Gym or open area

Skills

Striking • catching • dodging • fitness

Equipment

2 or more 8-1/2-inch gator-skin balls (coated foam ball) or plain foam balls

Activity

1. Players will begin play in a scattered formation.
2. Choose two or more players to be "it."
3. Give foam balls to the "it" players.
4. The objective of the game is for the "it" players to strike the ball with one hand in an attempt to make the ball tag other players.
5. Players with the ball are allowed to travel by tapping the ball with their hands, causing it to roll in an effort to get closer to others.
6. Players may dodge a ball that is struck at them, or they may try to catch it.
7. If a player fumbles the ball or is tagged by the ball, he or she must do three jumping jacks before returning to play.
8. Any player may obtain control of a loose ball and become "it."
9. Play is continuous and non-eliminating.

Variations

Make it easier:

Use one ball for a small group of fewer than six players, or use two or three balls for larger groups.

Make it more difficult:

Players can use their feet to side-kick balls; players must be stationary when kicking.

Adaptations

◎ Push students in wheelchairs if they are not mobile, or allow them to get out of their chairs if possible.

◎ Lead students who are blind or visually impaired with a tether, and give plenty of verbal cues.

Teaching Notes

◎ This is a great game for fitness.

◎ It also makes for a quick closing activity once the students learn the rules.

===TURKEY HUNT ===

Players

Small group

Area

Gym or open area with no obstacles, indoors or out

Skills

Fitness

Equipment

5 or 6 flag football flags

Activity

1. Choose one student to be the "turkey," and place the flags in his or her waistband or back pockets.
2. When you give the "go" signal, all other students (the hunters) will start chasing the turkey in an attempt to pull its tail feathers (flags).
3. Give the turkey a slight head start.

Variations

Make it easier:

- ⊙ Use fewer flags.
- ⊙ Use smaller boundaries.
- ⊙ Lead the turkey in groups of students with severe intellectual disabilities.

Make it more difficult:

Play Flag Tag (see page 34).

Adaptations

- Push students in wheelchairs if they are not mobile.
- Lead students who are blind or visually impaired with a tether.
- Assist students with severe intellectual disabilities.

Teaching Notes

- Everybody wants to be the turkey! My students love this game, and they run the entire time.
- Be aware that you need a lot of room for this game and need to remove any obstacles.

WORKING TOGETHER

Team-Building Games and Activities

The cooperative games and activities in chapter 4 are about *fun*. I recommend that you try these games to generate excitement and to motivate your students to move. The games may appear to be more developmentally appropriate for younger students, but they have proven successful for older moderate groups in my program. The games are not difficult to understand and provide opportunities for successful motor and social skill development.

Once again, modifications are included for games suitable for students with severe intellectual disabilities. Students with severe or profound disabilities may need hand-over-hand assistance or help to become mobile in a chair or ambulatory in a walker. Also, note that peer helpers or teacher assistants may be essential for success in these games. The recommended games for these students in chapter 4 are Volcano Eruption, Mud Pies, Team Beanbag (Treasure) Grab, Line Ball, and Noodle Balloon Volley.

All of the problem-solving and team-building activities are recommended for higher-functioning students with mild intellectual disabilities. The intent of these activities is to increase self-awareness through developing trust and respect for others.

BOUNCE AND SCORE

Players

Small or large group

Area

Gym or open area, indoors or out

Skills

Throwing • agility • tracking • teamwork

Equipment

4 cones for goal lines • 2 gator-skin balls • rope or spot markers
for boundary line

Activity

1. Set up a playing area with two parallel boundary lines approximately 20 to 30 feet apart to be used as goal lines.

2. Use a rope or spot markers to make a half-court boundary that students are not allowed to cross.

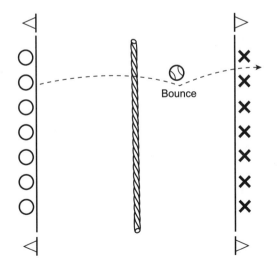

Bounce

3. Divide students into two teams and ask them to spread out along their designated goal lines. Students can move around to retrieve balls or to get closer to the half-court boundary to bounce the ball.

4. The objective as an offensive player is to throw the ball so that it crosses the opponent's goal line. However, the ball must bounce before crossing the line in order for the team to score.

5. The objective as a defensive player is to stop opponents' balls from crossing the boundary line. Students defending the goal line may use their feet, hands, or body in an attempt to stop the ball from crossing their goal line.

6. When a goal is scored, the game can continue or be restarted with a "go" signal.

Variations

Make it easier:

Use fewer balls if the students are having a difficult time tracking the balls.

Make it more difficult:

Use more balls with more advanced groups to increase the defense aspect of the game.

Adaptations

- ◎ Use bell balls for students who are blind or visually impaired.
- ◎ Use peer helpers or teacher assistants for students in wheelchairs and for students who are blind or visually impaired.
- ◎ Use only one ball for smaller groups.

Teaching Notes

This is a favorite game for my students. It's action packed and exciting.

=== BOX BALL ===

Players

Small or large group

Area

Gym or indoor open area

Skills

Agility • throwing • teamwork

Equipment

Mats or large boxes • 10 or more gator-skin balls • cones • tape or rope

Activity

1. Set up a playing area approximately half the size of a basketball court, with a center line. Use cones for the boundaries and tape or rope for the centerline.

2. Set up a goal on each back boundary line with several mats or large boxes. The goal should be about six feet by six feet and about three feet in height.

3. Divide the students into two groups, and assign sides for each group.

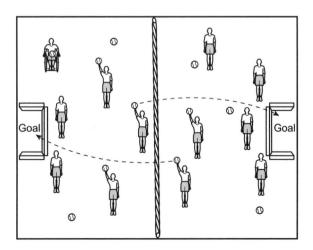

4. Each team starts with half the balls.

5. The objective of the game is to throw as many balls into the opponent's goal without crossing the center line.

6. Any player is allowed to block balls thrown by the opposing team.

7. Teams continue to play until all the balls are in the goals.

8. Count the number of balls in each goal to motivate teams to play harder, but do not worry about keeping score.

Variations

Make it easier:

Shorten the size of the playing area.

Make it more difficult:

⊚ Use more balls.

⊚ Use more goals.

Adaptations

⊚ Assist students who are blind or visually impaired.

⊚ Retrieve balls for students in wheelchairs.

Teaching Notes

⊚ This game is fast paced and fun. It is easy to understand and competitive enough to motivate all individuals involved.

⊚ This could be modified for some younger individuals or for lower-functioning groups. Use only one box (goal) in the center of play and have all students throw the balls into the box. Use music as a timer or motivating tool.

==== BUILD A SQUARE ====

Players

Small group

Area

Gym, classroom, or open area, indoors or out

Skills

Trust • teamwork • communication

Equipment

Rope • blindfolds

Activity

1. Explain to the students that they will be wearing blindfolds, with the exception of the leader. The leader is not allowed to speak during the activity.
2. The group's task (including the leader) is to form a square with a long rope while all the students are holding the rope.
3. Start the activity with all students standing in a line facing the rope. The rope should be lying parallel on the ground, approximately 15 feet from the group.
4. When you give the "go" signal, the group walks toward the rope.
5. You are responsible for monitoring that the students stay within the area to avoid walls or obstacles.
6. Remind the leader that he or she cannot talk, and ask him or her to figure out ways to communicate with others. Allow the leader to physically (and gently) lead students.

Variations

Make it easier:

If this seems too difficult, allow the leader to speak.

Make it more difficult:

If the students do this quickly, do not allow any players to talk.

Adaptations

Allow a student in a wheelchair to be the leader.

Teaching Notes

◎ Before starting, ask the group to choose a leader and discuss strategy.

◎ According to your group's ability level, add suggestions or ask questions that lead to discovery of better strategy.

◎ Remember that this is a cooperative activity, and some frustration can force the group to make decisions. If the frustration level gets too high, stop and debrief. Put-downs usually start when frustration is part of the picture.

◎ Choosing a leader can be difficult if the students all want to lead the group. Ask them to choose someone who has not been a leader in a previous activity.

◎ Debrief the activity.

  • What were your feelings or concerns?

  • How did you work as a group?

  • Can you make any changes that would help you with your next activity?

◎ This will prove to be a difficult activity for most groups. They will want to quit, and I suggest group discussion at this point.

◎ I also suggest performing this activity after completing other problem-solving activities first.

◎ This activity is recommended for students with mild intellectual disabilities.

Adapted from a Project Adventure Inc. workshop

▬▬▬ BUMPER BALL ▬▬▬

Players

Small or large group

Area

Gym or open area, indoors or out

Skills

Throwing accuracy

Equipment

Large therapy ball • at least 1 beanbag or small soft ball for each
student • rope or tape for boundary lines

Activity

1. Set up two boundary lines approximately 25 feet apart.
2. Divide the students into two teams, and ask them to start on a
   boundary line.
3. Place the large ball in the center of the two boundaries, and
   give each student at least one beanbag or ball.
4. When you give the "go" signal, the students will throw their
   beanbags or balls at the large ball in an attempt to force the ball
   over the opponent's boundary line.

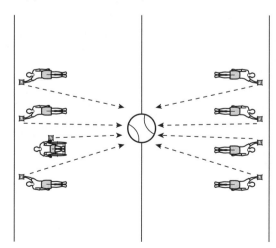

5. The students may leave the boundary line to retrieve their beanbags and continue throwing until one team has forced the ball over the opponent's boundary line.

6. Stress that no players are allowed to touch or kick the therapy ball. They may only throw beanbags at the ball. It is difficult for students with intellectual disabilities to understand the concept of proximity; therefore, I give them verbal reminders when they are too close to the bumper ball.

Variations

Make it easier:

⊙ Use a gator-skin ball for each student if you have enough of them.

⊙ For elementary students, start the therapy ball on one boundary line. All students try to force the ball over another line as a team.

Make it more difficult:

If you use balls to throw at the big ball, make the boundaries closer together and allow students to throw only from the boundary lines.

Adaptations

⊙ Use a large bell ball for students who are blind or visually impaired, and provide assistance.

⊙ Allow students in wheelchairs to start the game with more balls or beanbags. This can be accomplished by placing extra balls in a bag or bucket that is attached with Velcro to the chair.

Teaching Notes

⊙ It is very tempting for the students to touch or kick the ball, so be prepared to remind them often of this rule.

⊙ The students love this game but can at times become too aggressive.

CROCODILE WATERS

Players

Small group

Area

Gym, classroom, or indoor open area

Skills

Teamwork • trust • communication

Equipment

Scooter board • long rope • plastic bat • tape or rope for boundary lines

Activity

1. This cooperative activity develops teamwork because the students must work as a team to obtain their goal.

2. Set up two parallel boundary lines approximately 25 feet or more apart.

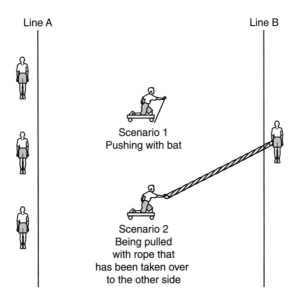

Line A

Line B

Scenario 1
Pushing with bat

Scenario 2
Being pulled
with rope that
has been taken over
to the other side

3. The objective of the activity is to get all players from one boundary line to the other without touching the floor or ground between the lines.

4. The group has been in a plane crash, and they are trying to find their way out of the jungle. They come to a crocodile river that they must cross.

5. The group is given a rope, a single-person raft (the scooter), and a paddle (the bat).

6. Players try to cross the river by pushing the raft with the paddle. Students who have reached the other side may help other players on the raft by pulling them with the rope, which one student must bring across (the rope needs to be longer than the distance between the boundaries). Any student may be pulled across once the rope has been taken over the river. Students will have to figure out how to get their supplies back to the starting boundary for those waiting to cross. You may need to help them discover ways to make this accomplishment.

7. If anyone touches the floor or ground in his or her attempt to cross, that person must return to the starting boundary line and make another attempt.

8. Hopefully, the students will ask this person to make a second attempt after others have had a first attempt. You may need to make this suggestion.

9. Remember to have the group discuss strategies before starting. For most groups this discussion will be teacher directed.

Variations

Make it easier:

Give the group clues. For example, if the students don't see that holding the rope above their heads would act as a cable for pulling themselves across, give them clues.

Make it more difficult:

Place obstacles in the river.

Adaptations

Allow students to help students in wheelchairs sit on the scooter, and disregard the floor rule for either player.

Teaching Notes

- ◎ This activity is fun and relatively easy.
- ◎ Larger students may need two scooter boards to cross, one to sit on and one for their feet.
- ◎ Your input should depend on the group's ability to problem solve.
- ◎ Monitor behavior and stop to discuss any put-downs or words of anger.
- ◎ The students can deal with some frustration, but do not let things get out of control.
- ◎ After the students have completed the task, discuss how the group worked together. Also, discuss any improvements that could help the group for the next activity.
- ◎ This activity is recommended for students with mild intellectual disabilities.

=== FOOT BALL ===

Players

6 to 12

Area

Open area, indoors or out

Skills

Communication • teamwork • focusing • problem solving

Equipment

Balls of various sizes (e.g., 24-inch beach ball, 10-inch playground ball, 8-1/2-inch playground ball, 5-inch playground ball, fleece ball)

Activity

1. Instruct the students to form a circle by sitting approximately elbow distance apart.
2. Inform the students that they may use only their feet in this activity.
3. The goal is to pass all of the balls consecutively around the circle in order of largest to smallest.
4. If any ball is dropped, the group must start over with that ball.
5. Choose one student to be the leader whose responsibility is to start the activity.
6. Allow the students to figure out the best solution for completing this task.
7. Students are allowed to pass more than one ball around the circle at a time.
8. Remember that you are more of a facilitator and should encourage the students to establish a plan and follow through.

Variations

Make it easier:

Allow students to use one hand to help pass the ball to the next person.

Make it more difficult:

Make the students pass the balls from smallest to largest.

Adaptations

- ⊙ If possible, allow students in wheelchairs to get out of their chairs. Let other students help them steady their legs if needed.
- ⊙ If students in wheelchairs cannot use their legs, then allow those students to use their hands.
- ⊙ Assist students who are blind or visually impaired with verbal cues.

Teaching Notes

- ⊙ This activity can cause some frustration, although most groups finish within one class period. Be patient with student frustrations and realize that this is part of the learning process.
- ⊙ Remind players that no put-downs are allowed or accepted.
- ⊙ Discuss the importance of having a leader and the other different roles of the group. Other roles include being a good listener or team player who is open to trying other people's ideas.
- ⊙ Discuss the group's feelings and what the group learned that may help them in the future.
- ⊙ This activity is recommended for students with mild intellectual disabilities.

Adapted from a Project Adventure Inc. workshop

==== GUARD THE PIN ====

Players

Small group

Area

Gym, classroom, or open area, indoors or out

Skills

Agility • throwing • teamwork

Equipment

Bowling pin • 8-1/2-inch gator-skin ball • rope or spot markers for circle boundary

Activity

1. Form a circle approximately 15 feet in diameter with rope or spot markers.
2. Place the bowling pin in the middle of the circle.
3. Appoint a student or ask for a volunteer to "guard" the pin. The objective is to keep the ball from hitting the pin.
4. All other players stand outside the circle and will attempt to hit the pin with the ball.
5. Any player who knocks the pin down with a thrown ball will become the new guard.
6. Discuss the strategy of passing the ball around the outside of the circle to other players in order to catch the guard unaware.
7. Allow accidental knockdowns. If the guard knocks the pin over when guarding it, reset and continue play.

Variations

Make it easier:

⊙ Allow the guard to stay in the circle for three knockdowns of the pin.
⊙ Allow the outside players to roll rather than throw the ball.

Make it more difficult:

- Use a larger circle.
- Use two or more pins.

Adaptations

- Place the pin at the top of the circle for the student guarding the pin in a wheelchair. All other students will stand at the bottom of the circle.
- Allow an extra guard for less skilled players.

Teaching Notes

The students often knock the pin down accidentally. Be prepared to reset often. Overall, the students love this game.

━━━ GUARD THE SQUARE ━━━

Players

Small or large group

Area

Gym, classroom, or open area

Skills

Throwing • reacting • teamwork

Equipment

8-1/2-inch gator-skin ball or sponge ball • rope for circle boundary • tape

Activity

1. Set up a large circle approximately 15 feet in diameter.
2. Using tape, make a square approximately 30 inches by 30 inches in the middle of the circle boundary.
3. Choose one player to stand inside the square as the guard.
4. All other players should stand outside the circle.
5. These players will attempt to bounce the ball in the square.
6. The player guarding the square may use his or her hands or feet to prevent the ball from bouncing in the square.

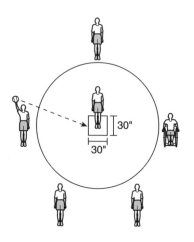

7. Remind players outside the circle that they may pass the ball to other players to try to catch the guard unaware.

8. Also, allow players guarding the square to stand in or out of the square.

Variations

Make it easier:

○ Allow the guard to continue guarding the square until the ball bounces two or three times in the square.

○ Allow more than one guard.

Make it more difficult:

With small groups, set up two smaller circles about 6 feet apart. Play a team version of Guard the Square. Players stand in both circles and try to throw beanbags or fleece balls into the square in the opponent's circle.

Adaptations

○ Use peer helpers or teacher assistants for students in wheelchairs who cannot spin themselves about.

○ Provide protective glasses for students who are blind or visually impaired.

Teaching Notes

○ The students in wheelchairs usually play this game very well.

○ All students seem to enjoy the game.

=== LINE BALL ===

Players

Small group

Area

Gym or open area

Skills

Striking • catching • teamwork

Equipment

8-1/2-inch gator-skin ball • tape or rope for boundary lines

Activity

1. Set up two parallel boundary lines approximately 15 to 20 feet apart.
2. Divide students into two teams and ask them to stand on the boundary lines facing each other.
3. The lines should be long enough to permit about 2 feet between each player standing on the line.
4. The objective of the game is to strike the ball with the hand, with the intent of forcing the ball over the opposing team's boundary line.
5. The students standing on the line try to gain control or stop the ball from crossing over the line.
6. Once a team stops the ball, that team tries to strike the ball over the opposite line. Students are not allowed to leave the line to strike the ball.
7. Play continues until a team scores. When you give the "go" signal, the team scored on strikes the ball again to restart play.

Variations

Make it easier:

⊙ Allow students to sit on the lines. Any balls above head level do not count as a score.

⊙ Allow students to kick the ball using the inside of the foot.

Make it more difficult:

Use two balls to speed up play and increase awareness.

Adaptations

⊙ If possible, allow students in wheelchairs to get out of their chairs and sit on the line.

⊙ Use bell balls for students who are blind or visually impaired.

⊙ When working with students with severe intellectual disabilities, use only one boundary line to strike the ball over. You may also place bowling pins on the line to give the game purpose.

Teaching Notes

⊙ Students appear to feel safe and unintimidated when playing this game.

⊙ They really enjoy sitting during this game.

===== MUD PIES =====

Players

Small or large group

Area

Gym or open area, indoors or out

Skills

Throwing • teamwork

Equipment

2 or 3 mats • fleece balls or foam balls

Activity

1. Place the mats upright in the center of the playing area. This represents the wall between two mud puddles.
2. Divide the players into two groups and scatter them about on either side of the wall.
3. Place balls randomly in each designated area.
4. When you give the "go" signal, the players will start throwing balls (mud pies) over the wall into the other group's area.
5. The objective of the game is to throw as many balls as possible over the wall before time expires.
6. Allow a minute or two for throwing.
7. Count the balls on each side if you feel this is necessary.
8. Reset, giving players time to rest and regroup.

Variations

Make it easier:

Play a noncompetitive game in which balls are not counted.

Make it more difficult:

⊙ Allow only underhand throws.
⊙ Allow only overhand throws.

Adaptations

⊙ Use peer helpers or teacher assistants for students in wheelchairs and for students who are blind or visually impaired.

⊙ Provide a bag or bucket for holding extra balls for students in wheelchairs and students who are blind or visually impaired.

⊙ Provide goggles for students who are blind or visually impaired.

⊙ Use peer helpers or teacher assistants to enable lower-functioning students to participate.

Teaching Notes

⊙ Beanbags are interchangeable for balls. Remember to use protective eye wear for students with visual impairments.

⊙ This game is easy for elementary students to understand.

⊙ It seems like chaos, but it is lots of fun.

==== NOD AND GO ====

Players

Small or large group

Area

Gym or open area, indoors or out

Skills

Communication

Equipment

Spot markers

Activity

1. Form a circle with spot markers, with one fewer spots than the number of students.
2. Instruct the group that there is no running in this game.
3. Explain that this is a game of communication without talking.
4. The objective of the game is for a student to change spots with another student.
5. Students will communicate with one another by nodding their heads.
6. The extra student will stand inside the circle and will try to obtain an open spot once others start changing spots.
7. The student left without a spot will go to the middle and try to obtain an open spot.
8. Play is continuous, with students attempting to change spots with the players they nodded to.
9. It is important for the students to understand that they cannot always exchange spots with the players they nodded to because others may get to those spots first. This actually adds to the risk taking.

Variations

Make it easier:

Add an exercise for the person left without a spot to slow down the pace of the game. Play would stop until the person in the middle does his or her assigned exercise. The teacher will possibly have to signal stop or make a rule that no one changes until the middle person has performed the exercise.

Make it more difficult:

- Use other exercises for the student in the middle.
- Use other means of communication (e.g., winking, foot tapping, clapping, eye contact).
- Remove an additional spot after a few minutes of play, resulting in more students in the middle.

Adaptations

- Make the circle larger to provide more room for students in wheelchairs.
- Assist students who are blind or visually impaired, and change the means of communication.

Teaching Notes

- Remember to discuss safety precautions before starting. You ultimately want the students to monitor safety.
- Usually the students will notice when the game becomes too aggressive and will ask for play to stop. If this happens, be sure to discuss what occurred and the changes that need to be made. The teacher can stop the game if play is getting too rough and students do not ask for it to stop.
- Possibly discuss feelings of fear or irritation concerning the rules being broken.

Adapted from a Project Adventure Inc. workshop

▬▬▬ NOODLE BALLOON VOLLEY ▬▬▬

Players

Small or large group

Area

Gym or open area

Skills

Hand–eye coordination • striking • strategy • teamwork

Equipment

Balloon • foam noodles (approximately 3 feet long) • pinnies to distinguish teams • tape or rope for boundary lines

Activity

1. Set up two parallel boundary lines approximately 20 feet apart.
2. Divide students into two teams.

3. One team will stand on each boundary line, each student holding a noodle.
4. Choose two players to start in the center to put the balloon in play.
5. Once the balloon is in play, all students may join the game.
6. The objective of the game is for each team to strike the balloon, causing it to cross over the opposing team's line.
7. This results in a score and a reset with two different players in the middle.

Variations

Make it easier:

Make smaller teams out of larger groups and rotate them in and out of play.

Make it more difficult:

- Discuss offense and defense.
- Allow only the two center players to move about; the line players sit on the line to protect it.

Adaptations

- Push students in wheelchairs if they are not mobile, or allow them to get out of their chairs if possible.
- Lead students who are blind or visually impaired with a tether.
- To modify for students with severe impairments, have everyone sit in a circle or on a mat and assist them in hitting the balloon with their hands.

Teaching Notes

- The students really love this game and are careful if safety is stressed.
- The foam noodles do not hurt students who are accidentally hit.
- I prefer playing this game with all students actively participating.

===ONE SQUARE===

Players

Small group

Area

Gym, classroom, or open area, indoors or out

Skills

Catching • tracking • competing • positive sports behavior

Equipment

8-1/2-inch gator-skin ball or 10-inch playground ball • tape or Velcro for boundary lines

Activity

1. Form a large square (4 feet by 4 feet or 6 feet by 6 feet) on the floor with tape or Velcro, depending on what type of floor covers the area of play.
2. Instruct one or two players to stand on each side of the square.
3. The objective of the game is to score a point by bouncing the ball in the square and forcing it to cross over one of the side-lines.
4. If the student on the side of the square catches the ball, there is no score and this student attempts to bounce the ball over one of the sidelines.
5. If a student fumbles the ball and the ball stays inside the square, there is no score.
6. However, if a student fumbles the ball and the ball crosses over the line, then the student who bounced the ball scores a point.
7. Remind all students to attempt to block the balls that they cannot catch.
8. Make two or more squares for larger groups.

Variations

Make it easier:

Use a smaller square.

Make it more difficult:

⊙ Count all fumbles as a score for more advanced groups.

⊙ Use a larger square.

Adaptations

⊙ Use bell balls for students who are blind or visually impaired.

⊙ Make the square smaller for students who are blind or visually impaired.

⊙ Use peer helpers or teacher assistants for students who are blind or visually impaired.

Teaching Notes

⊙ The students enjoy this game because it is easier to understand and to play than the original four-square game. Eventually, students may be able to play a typical four-square game.

⊙ At the end of the game, encourage the students to discuss the strategies they used (e.g., faking, high or low bounces).

=== RINGMASTER ===

Players

Small group

Area

Gym or open area

Skills

Throwing • dodging • teamwork

Equipment

8-1/2-inch gator-skin ball or sponge ball • rope for circle boundary • pinny

Activity

1. Form a large circle approximately 20 feet in diameter.
2. One student wearing a pinny stands in the middle and is called the ringmaster.
3. The ringmaster chooses another student to come inside the circle to be his or her guard.
4. All other players stand outside the boundary circle and will attempt to tag the ringmaster with the ball.
5. Remind the students to throw the ball at or below waist level.
6. Also, encourage the guard to try to protect the ringmaster by standing between the thrower and the ringmaster.
7. Whenever the ringmaster is hit, another ringmaster is chosen and he or she chooses a guard.

Variations

Make it easier:

⊙ Allow the ringmaster to be tagged two or more times before leaving the middle of the circle according to the student's ability level.

⊙ Allow two guards for some students.

Make it more difficult:

Specify that the ball must bounce before tagging the ringmaster.

Adaptations

- The ball must bounce before hitting a student in a wheelchair and can only hit his or her feet.
- Allow two guards for students who are blind or visually impaired.

Teaching Notes

- This is a very fun game for the students because they take a lot of pride in protecting others.
- Allow students to reflect on how they felt as the protector and how they felt as the person being protected.

= = = THE RIVER = = =

Players

Small group

Area

Open area, indoors or out

Skills

Problem solving • teamwork • trust

Equipment

Blocks of wood • tape or rope for boundary lines

Activity

1. Set up two parallel boundary lines approximately 25 feet apart, and give the students one fewer block of wood than the number of participants.
2. Explain that the space between the boundaries is a raging river.
3. Tell the students that they hit a huge rock and their boat split apart.
4. Pieces of the boat (blocks) are still floating in the river, and they have gathered the pieces.
5. They may use the pieces to cross the river. All team members must cross; no one can be left behind.
6. If a student steps off the block into the water, that student must return to shore and the team must figure out how to help them rejoin the group.
7. Another team member, usually the closest person to the block, may rescue the block.
8. Once a team member has crossed to the opposite shore, that student is not allowed to come back to help others or to rescue blocks. If that student takes a block to shore, the team may no longer use that block.
9. If the team uses up all the blocks before all members have crossed the river, the group starts over.

Variations

Make it easier:

- Allow several class periods for the group to finish.
- Modify rules that are too difficult for your group. For example, you can allow students to touch the water 2 or 3 times before having to start over.

Make it more difficult:

Set a time limit of 20 to 30 minutes.

Adaptations

- Allow students in wheelchairs to be pushed by students using blocks, but do not make both students start over if a mistake is made. Instead, allow the student in the wheelchair to wait for someone else to rescue him or her.
- Allow extra blocks for students who are blind or visually impaired. Team members who have already crossed the river can act as helpers, and these students do not need blocks.

Teaching Notes

- Allow time before the activity for discussion of strategies.
- Ask the students to think about the equipment and to think about the safest way to use it.
- The students will invariably try to slide across with the blocks, and they will make lots of mistakes. Be patient.
- If the students need direction, recommend a stepping stone strategy.
- You will also find yourself giving many clues for the problem-solving process. This will be more necessary for some groups.
- The students feel a great sense of accomplishment when finishing this activity and will probably cheer.
- This activity is recommended for students with mild intellectual disabilities.

Adapted from a Project Adventure Inc. workshop

STRIKER KICKBALL

Players

Small or large group

Area

Gym or outdoor open area

Skills

Striking • hand–eye coordination • teamwork

Equipment

Bases • lightweight ball or bladder ball

Activity

1. Divide students into two teams.
2. Set up the playing area for a kickball game, adjusting the distance between bases for students' skill level.
3. The rules are the same as for regular kickball, except the player strikes the rolled ball with his or her hand.
4. The student then attempts to run the bases.
5. Encourage defensive players to throw the ball to the base players when attempting to get a runner out.

Variations

Make it easier:

For groups who do not understand baserunning rules, allow runners to continue running even if they are tagged out.

Make it more difficult:

Alternate kicking and striking each turn at the plate.

Adaptations

⊙ Assist students in wheelchairs and students who are blind or visually impaired.

⊙ Allow students to stop the rolled ball before striking it.

⊙ Place the ball on a tee for students who are unable to strike a rolling ball.

Teaching Notes

The students love this version of kickball. Most students are successful at striking the rolled ball versus kicking the rolled ball.

▬▬▬ SURVIVE FOR FIVE ▬▬▬

Players

Small group

Area

Gym or open area

Skills

Throwing • teamwork

Equipment

Velcro vest with balls • Various objects (e.g., balls, rubber rings, cones) • rope, tape, or spot markers for boundary lines

Activity

1. Form a circle boundary or a boundary with parallel lines.
2. Scatter objects inside the boundary area.
3. The students should be positioned outside the boundary lines as a team.
4. One student, wearing the Velcro vest, will attempt to retrieve as many objects as possible from inside the boundary area before being hit five times (balls sticking to the vest) by the team.

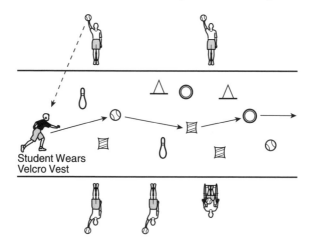

5. After five hits, a new player is chosen to retrieve objects from inside the boundary area.

6. The players participate as individuals and as a team.

Variations

Make it easier:

Allow two or more players to retrieve objects at a time.

Make it more difficult:

Use spot markers as safety bases for the retriever inside the boundary area to add a strategy condition.

Adaptations

⊙ Push students in wheelchairs if they are not mobile, and provide a gripper for picking up objects.

⊙ Allow another student to pick up objects and toss them to students in wheelchairs.

⊙ Allow students in wheelchairs to roll through the area without picking up objects.

⊙ Lead students who are blind or visually impaired with a tether, and help them pick up objects.

Teaching Notes

⊙ The students enjoy both roles of this game.

⊙ Discuss the role the students played as a team player and the role as an individual player. Ask which role they liked best and why.

⊙ Be sure to discuss any negative reactions to being hit when they occur.

⊙ This game is recommended for students with mild intellectual disabilities.

--- TARGET BASEBALL ---

Players

Small or large group

Area

Gym or indoor open area

Skills

Throwing • catching • teamwork

Equipment

Bases • target • Wiffle ball or 8-1/2-inch gator-skin ball

Activity

1. Set up the playing area for a kickball game.
2. Divide the students into two teams.
3. The offensive team will throw the ball at a target set up at the pitcher's mound.
4. An inflatable punching target that is weighted at the bottom and sets itself back upright when hit works well.
5. Each student is allowed as many throws as needed to hit the target.
6. Place the home plate closer in for students who find hitting the target difficult. Once the thrower hits the target, he or she runs the bases and the defensive team fields the ball.
7. After all offensive players have hit the target, the teams change places. Even if a player is thrown out at a base, allow that player to continue running the bases.

Variations

Make it easier:

Use a larger target.

Make it more difficult:

- ◎ Use small balls one day and larger balls another day.
- ◎ Adjust the target distance according to group throwing skills.
- ◎ Use the three-strike rule for more skilled groups.

Adaptations

- ◎ Adjust distances for students in wheelchairs, and allow them to go only to first base if their endurance is low.
- ◎ Use a bowling ramp for students in wheelchairs if they are unable to throw the ball.

Teaching Notes

- ◎ This game is just plain fun. The students love the inflatable target and get a kick out of hitting it.
- ◎ Do not worry about a lot of rules.
- ◎ Praise every throw.

--- TEAM BEANBAG (TREASURE) GRAB ---

Players

Small or large group

Area

Gym or open area, indoors or out

Skills

Agility • following directions • fitness

Equipment

Beanbags or various other objects • music • tape or spot markers for boundary lines

Activity

1. Set up two boundary lines 25 feet or more apart.
2. The sidelines of the gym are perfect boundaries.
3. Place the objects in a line or lines down the middle of the boundaries.
4. Divide the students into two teams and ask them to stand on the boundary lines.
5. When the music starts, students run to the middle and grab one piece of "treasure" (beanbag, ball) at a time.
6. Then the students run back and place the treasure on their boundary lines.
7. When all the treasure has been taken from the middle, stop the music and count the treasure for each team. Do not make a big deal out of the totals.
8. Have the students place the treasure back in the middle, then continue the game.
9. Be sure to remind the students that when the music is playing, it signals "go," and when the music stops, it signals "stop."

Variations

Make it easier:

⊙ Make the distance between the boundaries shorter.

⊙ When working with students with severe impairments, use only one boundary line and let the whole group collect bags as one team.

Make it more difficult:

Use different locomotor skills each time the game starts over (e.g., hopping, skipping, galloping, walking).

Adaptations

⊙ Push students in wheelchairs if they are not mobile, and allow them to use grabbers.

⊙ Place pieces of treasure closer to students in wheelchairs who choose to crawl.

⊙ Allow peer helpers or teacher assistants to lead students who are blind or visually impaired by the elbow or with a tether.

Teaching Notes

You really need to monitor some students, who may grab more than one treasure at a time. This is when the music comes in handy; just stop the music and remind everybody to take only one treasure at a time.

━━━ TREASURE CHEST ━━━

Players

Small group

Area

Gym or open area

Skills

Teamwork • agility

Equipment

24 beanbags • rope or spot markers for circle boundary

Activity

1. Form a circle boundary approximately 15 to 20 feet in diameter with a rope or spot markers.
2. Place all beanbags inside the circle.
3. Tell the students that the circle is a ship, then choose a volunteer to be the captain of the ship who guards the treasure of beanbags.
4. The remaining players, or pirates, stand on the outside of the ship.
5. All pirates then try to take the treasure.
6. If the captain tags a pirate when he or she enters the ship, the pirate must do three jumping jacks before attempting to take more treasure.
7. If a pirate has treasure in his or her hand when tagged while on the ship, the treasure must be left on the ship.
8. When all the treasure has been taken, assign a new captain.

Variations

Make it easier:

Allow two captains to guard the ship.

Make it more difficult:

Assign different exercises to pirates who are tagged.

Adaptations

- If possible, allow students in wheelchairs to get out of their chairs and crawl on gym mats.
- Allow students in wheelchairs to use grabbers.
- Allow students to toss the beanbags to students in wheelchairs; if a bag is dropped, it is placed back on the ship.

Teaching Notes

- Students love the metaphor of the ship and pirates. This seems to help them understand the game.
- Some students try to sit outside the boundary and reach for treasure. This should not be allowed for safety reasons.

--- VOLCANO ERUPTION ---

Players

Small or large group

Area

Gym or indoor open area

Skills

Throwing • teamwork

Equipment

3 to 4 mats • 25 to 50 soft balls (such as fleece or foam) • cones

Activity

1. Place the mats upright to form a circle that will be used as the volcano.
2. Choose two or more players to stand inside the volcano.
3. Place all the balls inside the circle of mats with the volcano players.
4. All other players should be scattered about the playing area outside the volcano.
5. To keep the players outside the volcano from getting too close, place a circle of cones around the mats. Otherwise, students tend to push or lean on the mats when throwing.
6. When you give the "go" signal, the players inside the volcano start throwing the balls out of the volcano.
7. The players on the outside will attempt to throw the balls back into the volcano.
8. Allow two to three minutes of throwing, then stop play.
9. Count the number of balls in the volcano if you wish to do so.
10. Change players in the volcano and start again.

Variations

Make it easier:

- Use fewer balls.
- Allow one to two minutes for throwing.
- With lower-functioning students, use assistants inside and outside the volcano to help throw the balls.

Make it more difficult:

Place the cones farther away from the volcano so that the throwers outside the volcano must make longer throws.

Adaptations

Use protective eye gear for students who are blind or visually impaired whether they are inside or outside the volcano.

Teaching Notes

- ⊙ This game provides repetition of throwing skills in a very fun manner.

- ⊙ Middle and high school students enjoy this game as much as elementary students.

- ⊙ Use newspaper rolled into balls and wound with masking tape to add weight if you do not have enough balls. You may also use beanbags, but remember to use protective eyewear for students with visual impairments.

- ⊙ Peer helpers or teacher assistants may be necessary when playing this game with students with severe intellectual disabilities.

CHAPTER 5

MOVING UP

Higher-Organization Games and Activities

The games in this chapter will help you challenge students who are ready to progress beyond the low-organization games found in chapter 3. Low-organization games focus on learning to play, learning to share, social skills, cooperation, having fun in a group, and being part of a team. They are easily understood and performed by most students. Often, once a basic skill is developed, you will want to present your students with a higher-organization game that will allow them to practice the learned skill.

Higher-organization games should be more challenging for students, present more than one objective, involve at least one rule and possibly timing, and reinforce learned skills. They should not be overly difficult to understand and should not prevent many students from being successful (either of these situations could lead to frustration and the urge to give up). They should be introduced when your students are ready to go a step beyond the simple games they've mastered.

There is a lot of overlap between higher-organization games and sport lead-up games. Please see chapter 6 for games that are entirely focused on sports skills. The games in chapter 6 are designed to help students learn one skill at a time, necessary for a specific sport, and ultimately progress to playing the actual sport. The games in chapter 5 may also prepare your students for lifelong sports and leisure participation, and this concept is emphasized in middle and high school adapted physical education, inclusive classes, or recreation programs. However, they are also fun games that will keep the students who are ready for them interested and challenged.

--- DOUBLE DRIBBLE BASKETBALL ---

Players

2 to 5 players per team (2 or more teams)

Area

Half the basketball court

Skills

Teamwork • dribbling • passing • catching

Equipment

Basketball • pinnies to distinguish teams

Activity

1. The game is played on one half of the basketball court. Extra teams can be alternated into play.
2. Play starts with a selected team on offense, with the players set up in positions such as point guards, wings (or guards), and post players (or forwards). The opposing team plays a person-to-person defense.
3. The objective of the game is to pass the ball around and eventually attempt a shot at the basket.
4. Players may take only two dribbles and then they must pass or shoot.
5. Players do not have to dribble before passing or shooting. However, the passing team must complete three passes before taking a shot or they pass as many times as they want before they shoot. The pass can be thrown in the air or bounced.
6. Made baskets count for two points.
7. Once the offensive team scores, the defensive team becomes the offense and resets as the original offensive team started.
8. Should the defensive team intercept a pass, they reset at the top of the key and become the offensive team.

Variations

Make it easier:

- ⊙ Use lower baskets.
- ⊙ Form teams with fewer players.
- ⊙ Use fewer passes.
- ⊙ Use smaller basketballs (the official women's ball).

Make it more difficult:

- ⊙ Do not allow any dribbling.
- ⊙ Add more passes.

Adaptations

- ⊙ Use spot markers to show students their starting positions on offense.
- ⊙ Allow students in wheelchairs to play without a defensive player, and physically help them move about and catch the balls.
- ⊙ Give lots of verbal cues to students unable to stay focused.

Teaching Notes

- ⊙ You will need to count the passes for the students.
- ⊙ Also, you may need to be available to receive a pass when teams cannot get the ball to other team members.

=== FACE-OFF ===

Players

Small group

Area

Open area, indoors or out

Skills

Agility • hand–eye coordination

Equipment

8 to 10 soft balls • tape or rope for circle boundaries • 2 bowling pins

Activity

1. The playing area is set up using two circles. The circles should be approximately 6 feet in diameter and about 10 to 12 feet apart.
2. Set a bowling pin at the back of each circle.
3. There will be one player in each circle to guard the pin.
4. The objective of the game is to knock down the pin in the opposing circle, which is being guarded by the opposing player.
5. Start the game with four or five balls in front of the player in each circle.
6. When you give the "go" signal, each player starts throwing balls at the opposing player's pin and attempts to block balls thrown at his or her own pin.
7. Use extra players to retrieve balls and roll them back into the circle in front of each player. If possible, use mats behind the circles to keep the balls in the playing area. In some indoor spaces, the walls may serve as these boundaries.

Variations

Make it easier:

⊚ Allow two players to guard each pin.

⊚ Set up the circles closer together.

⊚ Make the students roll the balls instead of throw them.

Make it more difficult:

Use fewer balls.

Adaptations

⊚ Use retrievers for students in wheelchairs, and allow them to get out of their chairs if they choose to.

⊚ Use peer helpers or teacher assistants for students who are blind or visually impaired and for students who do not understand the game.

Teaching Notes

⊚ My students love this game. They get as much enjoyment out of cheering for each other as they do out of playing.

⊚ They also love to choose the person they want to face off with.

=== HOTSHOT HOCKEY ===

Players

3 to 5 players per team (2 or more teams)

Area

Basketball court or outdoor field

Skills

Passing and shooting with a hockey stick • teamwork

Equipment

8 cones • tape or spot markers • pinnies to distinguish teams • softball-size Wiffle ball for the puck • hockey sticks

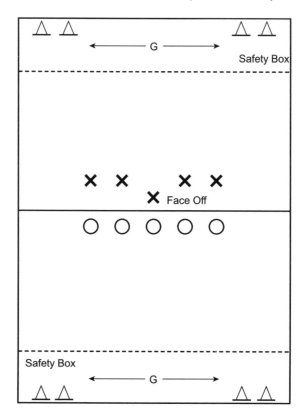

Activity

1. Divide the players into teams of two on two, three on three, or four on four, plus a goalie.
2. The playing area can be a basketball court or a slightly smaller outdoor field. Set up a goal (about 4 to 6 feet in width) in each corner of the field with the cones. Use tape or spot markers to mark a safety box for the goalie that extends across the entire end of the playing area, about 6 feet out from the goals. The goalie is responsible for defending both goals at his or her end of the court or field.
3. Play starts with a face-off in the middle of the playing area. This is a one-on-one situation with a player from each team. All players then try to score by shooting the ball into either goal in the end boundaries. The players are not allowed to enter the safety box to retrieve the ball or take a shot. The goalie roams between both goals. The goalie passes the ball out to a team-mate when the ball lands or is stopped in the safety zone.
4. Rough play or fouls result in a free shot for the player fouled.
5. When the ball goes out of bounds, players put the ball back into play with a pass from the sideline boundary.

Variations

Make it easier:

- ◉ Do not use goalies.
- ◉ Keep the number of field players small.
- ◉ Use a larger, slower ball as the puck.

Make it more difficult:

- ◉ Place a bowling pin in each goal and require that the pin be knocked down for a score.
- ◉ Assign a goalie to each goal.
- ◉ Make the goal smaller.

Adaptations

- ◉ Push students in wheelchairs if they are not mobile, and attach a hockey stick to their chairs or provide them with shortened sticks.

◎ Lead students who are blind or visually impaired by giving directional cues to help them figure out where they are on the court or field. When the ball comes to these students, stop the ball and allow the students to pass or shoot without a defensive player.

◎ Give constant directions and feedback to students who are confused.

Teaching Notes

Most children love to play hockey, and this game has been fun for my students.

=== ONE-BOUNCE VOLLEYBALL ===

Players

3 to 8 players per team (2 teams)

Area

Gym or outdoor open area

Skills

Hand–eye coordination • teamwork

Equipment

Volleyball net • volleyball • 4 cones for boundaries

Activity

1. Set up the volleyball court.
2. Divide players into two teams. If six to eight players make up each team, position the players in two lines, front and back.
3. Explain the rules much the same as for regular volleyball, with the following exceptions: the ball may bounce once before being played, and a player may catch the ball before volleying it back over the net. However, if the player drops the ball he or she is attempting to catch, a point is scored for the opposing team.

Variations

Make it easier:

- ⊙ Use softer balls or bladder balls.
- ⊙ Allow more space for students to move about by making smaller teams.
- ⊙ Allow players to throw the ball over the net instead of hitting or volleying it.
- ⊙ Allow servers to toss the serve over.
- ⊙ Play the game with all players tossing the ball over the net with no volleying.

Make it more difficult:

- Take away the bounce rule.
- Take away the catch rule.

Adaptations

- Toss the ball up for players in wheelchairs to hit, and help these students catch the ball.
- Allow another player to catch the ball for students in wheelchairs or any players having a difficult time receiving the ball. You may choose to give less skilled players the choice of receiving help or not.
- Help players who are blind or visually impaired to catch balls. Hold the ball for these students and allow them to hit the ball out of your hands. You may also allow these players to toss the ball to a sighted player, who will then hit the ball over the net.

Teaching Notes

Most players, when given the option, choose to catch the ball. Eventually, they attempt to volley the ball back over the net.

--- PARTNER MILE RUN ---

Players

Any size group

Area

Gym or outdoor open area

Skills

Fitness • flexibility • agility

Equipment

Cones to set up the track • fitness cards

Activity

1. Make fitness cards with different stretches, exercises, or stunts. If you use stretches, state an amount of time for each stretch. Exercises include jumping jacks, crunches, toe touches, leg raises, and push-ups.

2. Set up a running area about the size of a track field if possible. If you do not have a large outdoor area, make the track smaller.

3. Ask the players to choose a partner. You may need to supervise this task.

4. Inform the players that they will attempt to run or walk a mile together during the allotted time. One partner will run or walk around the track while the other partner does the activity on at least three cards. Once the first runner completes a lap, the players will change positions. This continues until a mile has been completed or a certain amount of time has expired.

Variations

Make it easier:

⊙ Make the track smaller.

⊙ Allow three members per partnership.

Make it more difficult:

- ☉ Increase the size of the track.
- ☉ Increase the number of laps or the time allotted.
- ☉ Add more difficult exercises to the cards.

Adaptations

- ☉ Push students in wheelchairs if they are not mobile.
- ☉ Lead students who are blind or visually impaired with a tether.
- ☉ Monitor any students with heart problems, and allow them only to walk.

Teaching Notes

My students seem to be more motivated to run when I assign them a partner. We even keep track of the mileage over a period of time and set goals for 25 or more miles as a group.

=== ROUNDBALL ===

Players

3 to 5 players per team (2 or more teams)

Area

Gym, multipurpose room, or outdoor open area

Skills

Throwing • catching • dribbling • teamwork

Equipment

2 large cones • 2 large playground balls • funnel or small plunger • pinnies to distinguish teams • 4 cones for boundaries • ball for passing • tape or spot markers

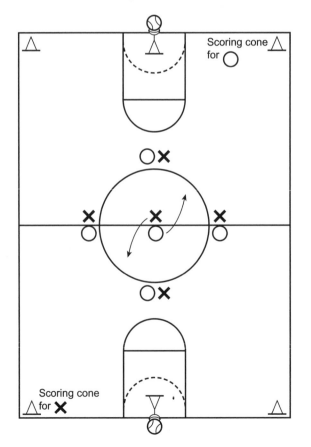

Activity

1. Set up the court using the basketball court boundaries, or use the cones. The size of the playing area will depend on the number of players. A field for 10 players would be larger than a field for 6 players. An estimated field size would be about 45 or 50 yards long and about 25 yards wide.

2. Set up a scoring cone in the middle of each end boundary line. Place a funnel or small plunger inside the cone to hold the bigger ball on top. To score a point, players must knock the ball off the opposing team's cone with the ball used for passing. Use tape or spot markers to designate an area that is a box or circle about 6 feet across that throwers are not allowed to enter when attempting to knock the ball off the cone.

3. Play starts with a jump ball at half-court.

4. The team gaining possession attempts to pass the ball to teammates working toward the scoring cone. The ball may be thrown in the air or bounced to teammates. Players may also dribble the ball to move forward.

5. No one may guard the scoring cone.

6. A turnover results when a team loses control of the ball or the ball goes out of bounds. The opposing team then becomes the offense and starts working toward the opposite goal. A throw-in is allowed for balls traveling out of bounds.

7. When a team scores by knocking the ball off the cone, the opposing team throws the ball in from the end boundary line.

Variations

Make it easier:

⊙ Allow the receiver of the pass to recover any ball thrown to him or her as long as it does not go outside the boundaries (no turn-overs).

⊙ Use fewer players on each team.

⊙ Do not allow the defense to block balls thrown by the offensive player. Only allow them to intercept passes. You may have to demonstrate this for your students.

Make it more difficult:

- ⊙ Take away the dribble option.
- ⊙ Make the no-enter zone larger.
- ⊙ Use a football as the throwing ball.

Adaptations

- ⊙ Catch the ball for students in wheelchairs and for students who are blind or visually impaired.
- ⊙ Use peer helpers or teacher assistants for students in wheel-chairs and for students who are blind or visually impaired.
- ⊙ Stop play to allow these same players to attempt to score.

Teaching Notes

You will need to monitor the no-enter zone. Someone will invariably try to guard the scoring cone.

▬▬▬ SAFETY ZONE FOOTBALL ▬▬▬

Players

6 or more

Area

Gym or outdoor open area

Skills

Throwing • catching • teamwork

Equipment

Football • pinnies to distinguish teams • 4 cones for boundaries • spot markers

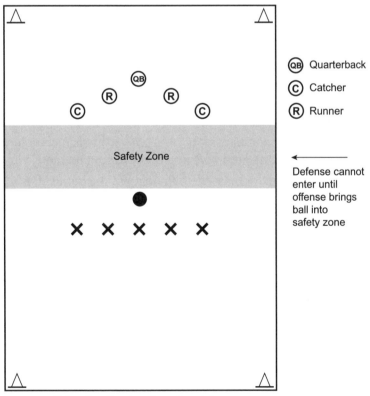

Set up for offensive play with a defense

Activity

1. Set up the football field.

2. Divide the group into two teams and assign positions to the players. You will need a quarterback, runners, and catchers (receivers) for the offensive team. Instruct the teams that when they do not have possession of the ball, they are on defense. Assign them players to guard.

3. Demonstrate how the teams should line up facing each other. The defensive team must line up in a straight line, across from the offense and out of the safety zone.

4. Inform the players that the defensive team cannot enter the safety zone (which is the space approximately 10 yards in front of the offensive line) until the offense has either run the ball to the safety zone line or thrown a pass to a player in the safety zone area.

5. A team is allowed four chances, or downs, to score before turning the ball over to the other team.

6. If the offensive team drops an attempted pass, play stops and a new down begins.

7. The defense needs only to touch the offense on the back to cause a new down. There is no tackling. Use flag belts instead if you have them.

8. You should adjust the safety zone area after each completed play, marking the area with one or more spot markers.

9. Throw-offs are made at the beginning of the game instead of kickoffs.

Variations

Make it easier:

○ Use smaller, lighter footballs.
○ Disregard the number of downs and allow the offensive team to continue play until someone scores.
○ You can play the quarterback position.

Make it more difficult:

○ Make the field larger for fitness purposes.
○ Make the safety zone area 5 yards.

Adaptations

- ◎ Players in wheelchairs may need help pushing their chairs, especially on an outdoor field. They may also need assistance catching the football, touching a player when playing defense, or grabbing the flag (if applicable).
- ◎ Lead students who are blind or visually impaired with a tether when running. Help them catch the ball, and assist them in playing defense by leading them and helping them pull the flag (if applicable).

Teaching Notes

- ◎ It may be necessary to ask students without disabilities to play the game with your groups if your students' skill levels and cognition are low.
- ◎ In a situation where students play three on three, the teacher will be the quarterback. For most of my groups, I am the quarterback for both teams.

━━━ TEAM HANDBALL ━━━

Players

4 to 6 players per team (2 teams)

Area

Gym or multipurpose room

Skills

Teamwork • throwing • catching • dribbling

Equipment

Playground ball or other high-bouncing ball • pinnies to distinguish teams • 4 cones for boundaries • tape

Activity

1. Set up the playing area (this game works best on an indoor basketball court or in a large multipurpose room). Use the boundaries of the court, or use cones to mark a large rectangular area in the multipurpose room. Use dark colored tape to make a square goal of about 6 feet by 6 feet directly on the wall. This square should be about 4 feet from the floor on each wall at the end of the court boundaries.

2. The objective of the game is for a team to move the ball down the court in an effort to shoot at the goal (throw the ball into the square, which is defended by a goalie) for a point. To move the ball down the court, players are allowed to dribble or to pass to a teammate.

3. When a shot is taken, play continues if the ball rebounds back into the court area. If the ball rebounds outside the boundaries, the defensive team is allowed to inbound the ball from the sideline and becomes the offensive team.

4. Many rules are the same as for basketball. Play starts with a jump ball in the center court area. If the offensive team loses the ball out of bounds, the defensive team takes control and becomes the offensive team. The defensive team also gains possession when intercepting passes.

5. Rough play or fouls result in free shots for the player in possession of the ball. A free shot is taken from the free-throw line against the goalie.

Variations

Make it easier:

- ◎ Do not use goalies.
- ◎ Divide the players into smaller teams to allow more open space for passing and dribbling.
- ◎ Tape the goal closer to the floor, and add a rule that requires the ball to bounce before entering the goal.

Make it more difficult:

- ◎ Use more than one goalie for each team.
- ◎ Make the goal smaller.

Adaptations

- ◎ Teach students in wheelchairs to dribble by holding the ball in their laps while pushing the chair; they may need assistance in pushing.
- ◎ Lead students who are blind or visually impaired with a tether. Give constant verbal cues or assign a peer helper.
- ◎ Give verbal cues to help keep students with autism on task.

Teaching Notes

You should be prepared to give constant cues to direct the players to the correct goals.

=== THREE ON THREE ===

Players

3 players per team (2 or more teams)

Area

Gym or outdoor open area

Skills

Teamwork • fitness

Equipment

Soccer ball, hockey sticks, or Pillo Polo set • pinnies to distinguish teams • 4 cones

Activity

1. Decide whether you want your students to play soccer, hockey, or Pillo Polo. Then, set up a playing field using the boundaries of the basketball court in the gym or a large area outside. Set up a goal at each end with cones.
2. Divide the group into teams of three, two field players and a goalie.
3. Play starts in the middle of the playing area, with one team on offense and one team on defense.
4. The teams are smaller than typical sports teams; therefore, all players have a better opportunity to participate.
5. Determine the safety rules needed for each sport.

Variations

Make it easier:

⊙ Play with only one field player per team, or do not use goalies.
⊙ Use a smaller field area.
⊙ Use a beach ball or gator-skin ball as the hockey puck for groups with lower skill levels.

Make it more difficult:

Use a smaller goal.

Adaptations

⊙ When playing soccer, allow students in wheelchairs to carry the ball.

⊙ Push students in wheelchairs if they are not mobile.

⊙ Use peer helpers or teacher assistants for students who are blind or visually impaired.

Teaching Notes

⊙ My students always feel that they have played a soccer or hockey game when I divide them into three-on-three teams.

⊙ Everyone gets lots of playing time and skill development.

⊙ Teamwork is easier with fewer players on the field.

⊙ The students really start comprehending the transition of offense and defense.

---- ULTIMATE FRISBEE ----

Players

2 to 8 players per team (2 or more teams)

Area

Gym or outdoor open area

Skills

Throwing a Frisbee • catching • teamwork

Equipment

3 to 5 Frisbees for each team • pinnies to distinguish teams • 4 cones for boundaries • target

Activity

1. Set up the field area, approximately 50 to 75 yards by 25 yards, or use the gym. Add a target to the end line. Some suggestions include a soccer goal, a large trashcan, or a large box. You may need to place the trashcan or box on its side for players with lower skills.
2. Divide the group into two teams.
3. Each team starts on an opposite end boundary line with three to five Frisbees, but players can throw only one Frisbee at a time.
4. The objective of the game is to make at least three (or more) successful passes and then attempt to throw the Frisbee into a target. Once the initial three passes have been made, allow as many attempts as needed to throw the Frisbee into the target.
5. A player must successfully catch the Frisbee before throwing it to another player downfield toward the goal-line target.
6. If the Frisbee goes outside the boundaries, the thrower retrieves it and passes it to another player.
7. This is basically a competition between the two teams to see who can score with all their Frisbees first.
8. Allow the teams to come up with a strategy before playing the game. Some teams will need to make short passes, and some teams will be able to make longer passes.

Variations

Make it easier:

- ⊙ Make the field shorter.
- ⊙ Allow drops to count as completed passes as long as the Frisbee touched a team member's hands.
- ⊙ You can be the only thrower (somewhat like a quarterback).

Make it more difficult:

- ⊙ Use a larger field.
- ⊙ Allow one team member from opposing teams to play defensively and try to deflect the passes.
- ⊙ Add more Frisbees.

Adaptations

- ⊙ Push students in wheelchairs if they are not mobile, and help them catch the Frisbee if needed.
- ⊙ Lead students who are blind or visually impaired with a tether, and catch the Frisbee for them. Also, toss these students the Frisbee by giving verbal cues such as "Ready" and "Catch," and help them throw the Frisbee to a teammate.

Teaching Notes

The players will usually attempt longer passes with little success. You may need to stop play to point this out and help them determine whether it would be easier for their team to complete shorter passes.

CHAPTER 6

LIFETIME FITNESS

Lead-Up Sport and Leisure Games and Activities

The activities in this chapter are more complex drills designed to improve sports skills for older students and athletes who are intellectually disabled. As an adapted physical educator and Special Olympics coach, I have observed that my students and athletes lack certain skills that seem automatic or natural to their peers without disabilities. For example, jumping for the rebound in basketball, sprinting for the loose ball in soccer, moving to an empty space to receive a pass, or other basic team strategies are sometimes deficient.

The drills included in this chapter are designed to reflect game situations. The drills consist of multiple-step fundamental skills presented in easy-to-understand directions. However, as teacher or coach, you must be the director, giving constant feedback and reminders. It is somewhat like play-by-play action.

In my working experience, basketball has proven a more popular sport for my athletes; therefore, I have included more developmental activities for this advanced sport. The soccer activities in this chapter can also be interchanged or set up for the sport of hockey. The lead-up games are designed to develop teamwork as well as fundamental skills. They can serve as a culminating activity or as a step toward more competitive play for higher-functioning athletes.

The idea behind these games is to teach essential skills, chain the skills together, and eventually lead students toward sports or sportlike activities. Because encouraging lifetime physical activity is one of the goals of both traditional and adapted physical educators, teaching sports skills and progression should not be reserved for certain students only. Students with intellectual disabilities will benefit from developing sports or leisure skills and ideally, like other students, will carry the learned behavior into adulthood and beyond.

An example of a progression of skills into a lifetime sports or leisure activity is exemplified in the book *Sport Progressions* (Clumpner 2003). One part of the book is devoted to developing a golf game, step by step. The skill development begins with imaginary putting (with a large target or no target) and progresses to putting following a line or carpet strip, then putting to a target, playing miniature golf, chipping a Wiffle ball, driving balls off a mat, and driving balls off a tee, with the eventual goal of playing nine holes of golf. This type of progression plan is useful for all physical educators, and the games in this chapter can help you develop similar programs.

▬▬▬ 30-SECOND DRILL ▬▬▬

Players

Small or large group

Area

Gym or outdoor court

Skills

Shooting

Equipment

Basketball

Activity

1. This is a timed shooting drill (30 seconds) in which the player starts shooting from the block and continues to shoot until time expires.
2. The shooter will rebound his or her ball.
3. This drill is designed to help players use the box on the backboard.
4. When time expires, the next person in line becomes the new shooter.

Variations

Make it easier:

Adjust the time allowed for shooting. Less time means that the student doesn't have to keep trying to make as many shots.

Make it more difficult:

Use spot markers to set up the drill around the lane area.

Adaptations

Add a person to rebound for players needing assistance.

Teaching Notes

This is a great opportunity to reinforce using the backboard, and it also helps with timing when rebounding.

━━━ BALLOON SOCCER ━━━

Players

Small group

Area

Gym or multipurpose room

Skills

Teamwork • kicking • fitness

Equipment

2 hula hoops • 1 balloon • pinnies to distinguish teams • 4 cones for boundaries

Activity

1. Set up a rectangular playing field approximately 12 feet by 20 feet. Team A wears pinnies and stands along one sideline; team B will stand on the opposite sideline.

2. One student from each team will stand on the end lines and will play the hoop helper position.

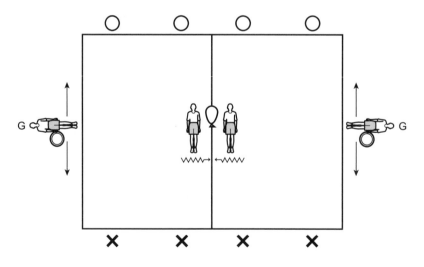

3. The hoop helpers will hold a hula hoop as the goal for kicking the balloon through, and they are allowed to move the hoop from side to side to enable the balloon to pass through. All other students are assigned a number that corresponds with the opposing team.

4. When a student's number is called, the student enters the playing area and will play one-on-one soccer with the opposing student with the same number.

5. Play continues until one of the players scores by kicking the balloon through the hoop.

6. You announce, "Score," and call another number for a pair of students to enter the playing area.

7. The students standing on the boundary lines help keep the balloon in play by kicking out-of-bounds balloons back into the playing area.

8. Sideline players are not allowed to enter the playing area until their number is called for one-on-one play.

Variations

Make it easier:

◎ Allow extra hoop helpers.

◎ Adjust boundaries according to the number of students.

◎ You or a teacher assistant can hold the goal hoops to help students score when needed.

Make it more difficult:

◎ Allow students to play two on two or three on three.

◎ Increase the size of the playing area.

Adaptations

◎ Use peer helpers or teacher assistants for students in wheelchairs.

◎ Allow students in wheelchairs to use foam noodles to hit the balloon.

Teaching Notes

- This game is easy and safe as long as you allow only one or two players from each team inside the playing area for higher-functioning students. It is possible to play three on three with lower-functioning and nonaggressive groups.
- It is great for improving fitness levels.
- I usually announce, "Score," but I do not worry about a tally of the score.
- The objective is to give all students the opportunity to score at some point during the game.

— — BALLOON VOLLEY — — —

Players

Small or large group

Area

Gym or indoor open area

Skills

Cooperation • hand–eye coordination

Equipment

Balloons

Activity

1. Students stand facing a partner or in a circle facing the middle.
2. The objective of the game is for students to keep a balloon in the air by tapping it with their hands back and forth to a partner or to teammates.
3. Students can then try tapping the balloon with their feet only.
4. After a few minutes of practice, allow students to count consecutive taps that keep the balloon suspended in the air.

Variations

Make it easier:

- Tether the balloon to any student unable to track and tap the balloon.
- Use a beach ball instead of a balloon.

Make it more difficult:

- Use a net for the students to tap the balloon over (if no net, use rope).
- Make students sit on the ground when tapping the balloon over the net.
- Make students hold hands to form a circle and attempt to keep the balloon suspended in the air.

Adaptations

- Use partners for students in wheelchairs if needed.
- Tether the balloon for students who are blind or visually impaired.

Teaching Notes

- **Do not use latex balloons with students who are allergic to latex.**
- This is a good activity for students who find striking or tracking objects difficult. The balloon floats and allows more time for students to react or respond.
- This is a good lead-up activity for participation in a volleyball game.
- A good follow-up activity is a balloon tap relay:
  - Organize the students in relay lines.
  - The students tap the balloon down to a line and run back with the balloon in their hands.
  - Students may also kick the balloon relay style.

BASEBALL PIN BALL

Players

Small group

Area

Gym or open area

Skills

Hand–eye coordination • turn taking • aiming • force

Equipment

Large plastic bat • tee or large cone • sponge ball • 4 bowling pins

Activity

1. This is a skill development activity.
2. When students are not practicing the skill, they will be waiting for their turns.
3. Line up the bowling pins approximately 12 to 14 inches apart.
4. Set up a batting tee or cone approximately 6 to 8 feet parallel to the pins.
5. The students will take turns hitting the sponge ball off the tee or cone in an attempt to knock the pins down.
6. Allow each student at least four attempts before the next student comes up to bat.
7. Stress soft force for hitting and adjusting the stance for aiming at the pins.
8. For groups with more than four students, it is recommended to set up extra batting tees to reduce wait time.

Variations

Make it easier:

Use more pins.

Make it more difficult:

Use fewer pins.

Adaptations

- ⊙ Use hand over hand for students who are unable to swing the bat alone and for students who do not understand.
- ⊙ Use more verbal cues for students who are blind or visually impaired, and use hand over hand for these students if necessary.

Teaching Notes

- ⊙ This game is recommended for younger or lower-functioning individuals.
- ⊙ My younger students enjoy and understand this game because the rules are simple.
- ⊙ This type of activity reinforces turn taking and sharing.

━━━ BASKETBALL SHUFFLE ━━━

Players

Small or large group

Area

Gym or open area, indoors or out

Skills

Passing • shooting • focusing

Equipment

Playground ball or basketball • goal • music

Activity

1. Instruct all students to stand in a circle.
2. Give one student the ball to start the passing action.
3. When the music starts playing, the players pass the ball around the circle in sequence by handing the ball to the person standing next to them.
4. When the music stops, the student holding the ball will dribble or walk to the goal and shoot.
5. Allow the shooter to continue until a basket is made.
6. When the student returns to the circle, start the music so that the game can continue.

Variations

Make it easier:

- ⊙ Allow students to sit while passing the ball; many students need to build the necessary leg strength and balance required to go from a seated position to a standing position.
- ⊙ Keep score as a team.

Make it more difficult:

- ⊙ Adjust the height of the goal.
- ⊙ Assign designated shooting spots.

Adaptations

- ☉ Use a lower or modified goal for elementary students, students in wheelchairs, and students who are blind or visually impaired.
- ☉ Use spot markers to help elementary students form the circle.

Teaching Notes

- ☉ The students tend to stay focused in anticipation of the music stopping when they have the ball.
- ☉ Elementary students feel as if they actually played a basketball game when they are finished.

▄▄▄ BUMPER POOL ▄▄▄

Players

Small or large group

Area

Gym, classroom, or open area

Skills

Rolling accuracy • force • strategy

Equipment

8 to 10 lightweight balls of varying sizes • rope or tape for circle boundary • 5-inch playground ball

Activity

1. Form a circle approximately 10 to 15 feet in diameter with rope or tape.
2. Place the lightweight balls inside the circle.
3. Provide a 5-inch playground ball as the "bumper" ball.
4. Instruct the students to take turns rolling the bumper ball at the pool balls inside the circle in an attempt to bump the balls out of the circle.
5. A student receives a point per ball that he or she bumps out with the bumper ball.

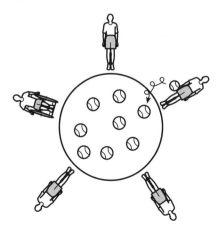

6. Allow the students to move around the circle for better positioning.

7. Once all balls are out of the circle, reset and start again.

Variations

Make it easier:

Do not worry about keeping score, just continue taking turns.

Make it more difficult:

- Keep score as a team.
- If the bumper ball stays in the circle after forcing a pool ball out of the circle, the player gets another roll.

Adaptations

- Allow students in wheelchairs to get out of their chairs if possible.
- Provide an instrument (e.g., hockey stick) for students in wheelchairs to push the ball with if they have difficulty rolling.
- Provide a ramp for rolling.

Teaching Notes

- Set up two circles for large groups, especially with the middle or high school levels.
- You can see the students plan and use strategy.
- This is a slow game, but all ages seem to enjoy it very much.

=== CIRCLE BOWLER ===

Players

Small group

Area

Gym or open area

Skills

Rolling • aiming • fitness • following rules • turn taking

Equipment

Spot markers • lightweight bowling pin • 10-inch playground ball

Activity

1. Form a circle with the spot markers, and ask each student to stand on a spot.
2. Place a bowling pin in the center of the circle.
3. Instruct the students that they will take turns rolling the ball at the pin in an attempt to knock the pin down.
4. Once a student knocks the pin down, he or she will run around the outside of the circle and then return to his or her position.

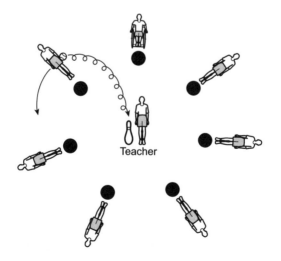

Teacher

5. During the run, the teacher should stand in the middle of the circle and count out loud while bouncing the ball at a high level.

6. Instruct the students that they are trying to get back to their positions before you finish counting to a certain number (10 or 15).

7. You may need to stall to give some students ample time to return to their spots.

8. Once a student returns to his or her spot, everybody celebrates (claps).

Variations

Make it easier:

◎ Allow more attempts to hit the pin.

◎ Place more pins in the middle of the circle.

Make it more difficult:

Make the circle larger.

Adaptations

◎ Push students in wheelchairs if they are not mobile.

◎ Provide an instrument (e.g., hockey stick) to help students in wheelchairs who are not flexible enough to lean over to roll the ball, or use a bowling ramp.

Teaching Notes

◎ This game is more appropriate for younger students or lower-functioning students. Most students will need prompting to get started with their run. You may need to lead some students through the whole game.

◎ The spot markers are necessary to help them return to their positions.

◎ Ultimately, this game could lead students toward a lifelong interest in bowling. When students are ready, let them work on rolling the ball in a straight line toward an individual target (more like a bowling alley). Eventually you may be able to take them on a class trip to a local bowling alley. Most will accommodate any special needs for your students, including providing ramps and bumpers.

= = = CIRCLE PASS = = =

Players

Small or large group

Area

Gym or outdoor open area

Skills

Passing • faking • pivoting • defending the pass

Equipment

Basketball

Activity

1. Instruct the players to form a large circle, with one volunteer player in the middle as the defender. The players in the circle should be spaced at least 3 feet apart.
2. The circle players will pass the ball around in an attempt to keep the defender from obtaining the ball.
3. Before play starts, teach all players how to fake left or right with the ball in their hands, to pivot left or right to step around the defense if needed, and to use head fakes.
4. Teach the defender how to step into the passing lane when the ball is thrown from player to player.
5. After 10 or more passes, allow another volunteer to become the defender.

Variations

Make it easier:

◎ Use more circles for larger groups.
◎ Use two defenders in the circle if needed.

Make it more difficult:

◎ Designate the type of pass to be used.
◎ Designate right- or left-hand passes.

Adaptations

Allow for a larger personal space for students in wheelchairs. Spot markers may be helpful to prevent the defenders from getting too close and standing over students in wheelchairs.

Teaching Notes

⊙ This drill is a great practice situation for teaching the passer to pivot around the defense, which is often difficult to remember.

⊙ The defender learns how to follow and track the ball as if in a zone defense situation.

=== DRIBBLE AND JUMP STOP DRILL ===

Players

Small or large group

Area

Gym or outdoor court

Skills

Dribbling • ball handling • stopping with control

Equipment

Basketballs

Activity

1. Instruct the players to line up on an end boundary line.
2. The number of dribblers depends on the number that you feel comfortable watching.
3. When you give the "go" signal, the players will start dribbling.
4. When you give the "stop" signal, the players will stop and jump with a one-foot takeoff and a two-foot landing, feet parallel to each other.
5. Tell the students to focus on the jump technique and also on holding the ball with two hands.
6. Continue to the opposite end of the court, giving three or four stopping opportunities.

Variations

Make it easier:

Dribble alongside the players, acting as a visual cue.

Make it more difficult:

Add pivoting (keeping the ball of the foot on the ground while stepping with the other) once the players can jump stop on two feet.

Adaptations

- ⊙ Help students in wheelchairs to stop.
- ⊙ Teach students in wheelchairs to dribble (one dribble per three pushes).

Teaching Notes

This is one of the most important skills to teach players for ball control and can be incorporated into many other drills. I use this drill often at the beginning of basketball season.

▬▬▬ DRIBBLE, PASS, AND SHOOT ▬▬▬

Players

Any size group

Area

Gym, outdoor open area, or soccer field

Skills

Dribbling • passing • shooting

Equipment

Soccer balls • 2 cones

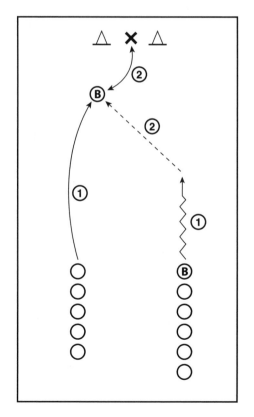

Activity

1. Set up the goal area with the cones approximately 6 feet apart.
2. Arrange the players in two lines, one for dribbling and passing, and the other for receiving and shooting. Space the lines about 10 yards apart.
3. The player in the dribbling line starts with the ball and dribbles four or five times before passing to the receiver, who is running down the field parallel to the dribbler.
4. Once the receiver gets the ball, he or she takes a shot at the goal or dribbles closer to take the shot.
5. The players return to the ends of the lines, switching positions. You will initially need to verbally cue the players to help them with their timing.
6. Before beginning this activity, demonstrate how to kick a leading pass and how to receive the ball with the inside of the foot.

Variations

Make it easier:

Let the players start from stationary positions, and allow them to just pass and shoot.

Make it more difficult:

- Add a goalie.
- Add a defensive player.

Adaptations

Assist any players having problems passing and receiving.

Teaching Notes

This drill teaches the players how to work together and how important it is to pass.

▪▪▪ FOUR CORNER GOALIE ▪▪▪

Players

Any size group

Area

Gym, outdoor open area, or soccer field

Skills

Kicking • blocking

Equipment

Foam balls or soft balls • 8 cones

Activity

1. Start with an area large enough for a square space approximately 25 feet by 25 feet. Use cones to set up four goals, about 10 feet wide, one on each side of the square.

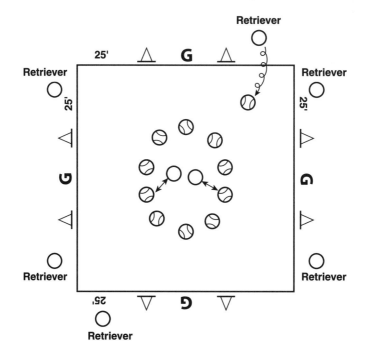

2. Place at least eight or more balls in the center of the square, and allow one or two players to come to this area as the kickers. Allow goalies in each goal area.

3. When you give the "go" signal, the kickers start kicking at any goal and continue until a designated time has expired.

4. Extra players should retrieve balls and roll them back into the middle of the playing area for the kickers.

5. After time expires, rotate new players in as goalies and kickers. Use foam balls or soft balls if possible for this drill because balls will be flying everywhere.

Variations

Make it easier:

Do not use goalies.

Make it more difficult:

Adjust the size of the playing area to make it larger.

Adaptations

Physically assist goalies with severe delayed reactions.

Teaching Notes

⊙ This drill is basically controlled chaos.

⊙ The players love it, and it teaches them to shoot quickly.

▪▪▪ FRISBEE PIN BALL ▪▪▪

Players

Small group

Area

Gym or open area, indoors or out

Skills

Throwing accuracy with Frisbees

Equipment

2 Frisbees for each student • rope for circle boundary • 10 bowling pins • spot markers or hula hoops

Activity

1. Form a large circle approximately 15 feet in diameter with a rope.
2. Set up the bowling pins on the inside of the circle boundary.
3. Place spot markers or hula hoops outside the circle at varying distances.
4. The objective of the game is to knock down the pins with thrown Frisbees.

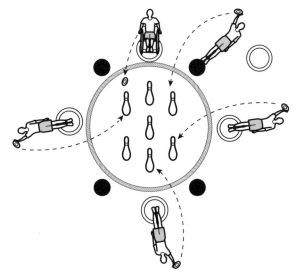

5. The students may throw only from a spot marker or hoop.

6. After throwing their Frisbees, students retrieve them and continue throwing from the spots or hoops until all pins are down.

7. Reset and start a new game.

8. Putting a time limit on the game usually motivates the students to stay focused. I suggest two minutes.

Variations

Make it easier:

Do not use spot markers or hoops outside the circle.

Make it more difficult:

For more skilled groups, allow the students to guess how long it will take them to knock down all the pins. Then each game afterward, challenge the students to improve their time.

Adaptations

◎ Use retrievers for students in wheelchairs, or give them more Frisbees at the beginning of the game.

◎ Give verbal cues to students who are blind or visually impaired.

Teaching Notes

◎ Throwing skills improve greatly with this game.

◎ Students become more accurate and more focused.

◎ Throwing a Frisbee is a great leisure activity that students can enjoy as adults.

=== JUMP, STOP, AND SHOOT ===

Players

Small or large group

Area

Basketball court

Skills

Jump stop • dribbling • shooting

Equipment

Basketball

Activity

1. Form a line at half-court, and give the first player a ball.
2. The player dribbles down to the block (the black box on the side of the free-throw lane), jump stops, then shoots using the backboard. The two-foot jump stop will help the shooter with ball control.
3. Shooters need constant reminders to use the backboard.
4. The shooter retrieves the ball and throws it back to the next person in line.
5. He or she then returns to the back of the line by running around the opposite side of the court.

Variations

Make it easier:

Use no dribble, and start the drill at the box.

Make it more difficult:

Make the shooters stop at different spots around the lane (right or left elbow, free-throw line, or in front of the basket).

Adaptations

⊙ Help students in wheelchairs with stopping and ball control.

⊙ Use lower baskets for students in wheelchairs.

⊙ Use spot markers for shooting positions.

Teaching Notes

This drill reinforces better ball-handling skills as well as develops shooting skills.

━━ LAYUP DRILL ━━

Players

Small or large group

Area

Basketball court

Skills

Dribbling • layup shooting • passing

Equipment

Basketballs • 2 cones

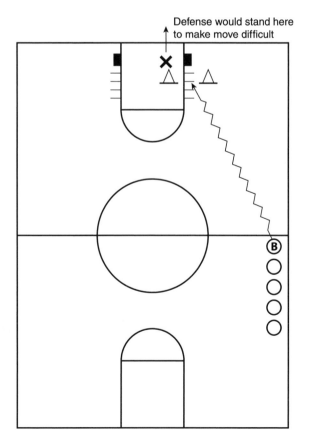

Defense would stand here to make move difficult

Activity

1. Place the cones about 3 feet apart between the second and third hash marks on the free-throw line. Call this the "gate."
2. Explain and then demonstrate to the players that they must go through the cones before shooting their layups.
3. Point out, if possible, that they will try to pick the ball up from the dribble at the gate and take a step before shooting.
4. After the shot, the player will get his or her own rebound and pass the ball to the next person in line.
5. If you choose to use two balls, then the second person in line will start dribbling as soon as the first player gets the rebound. The student who rebounds would then pass to the next person in line without a ball.

Variations

Make it easier:

Make the "gate" wider.

Make it more difficult:

Assign a defensive player to block the offensive shot.

Adaptations

- Lower the basket for students in wheelchairs.
- Use a beeper on the backboard for students who are blind or visually impaired.

Teaching Notes

- Emphasize going through the gate to provide a better angle for the shot.
- The footwork will improve with practice.
- This drill also provides much needed dribbling practice.

═══ LAYUP FROM PASS ═══

Players

Small or large group

Area

Basketball court

Skills

Dribbling • passing • layup shooting

Equipment

Basketballs • spot markers

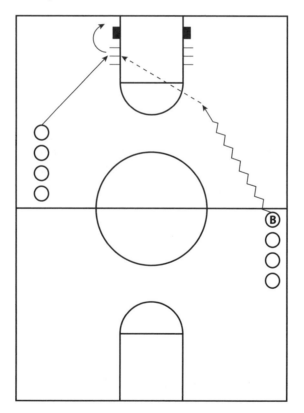

Activity

1. Divide the students into two lines, passers and shooters. The passers will line up at half-court in the center circle. The shooters will line up on the right or left side near the boundary line, about 6 feet closer in than half-court. You will probably need spot markers for the starting points.

2. When you give the "go" signal, the passer takes about two dribbles and then passes to the shooter, who is heading for the basket. The shooter receives the pass and shoots a layup.

3. Explain and demonstrate that the passer must throw a leading pass to the shooter. This leading pass should be in front of the shooter so that the shooter can continue in a forward motion and take a shot.

4. The shooter gets the rebound and dribbles on the opposite side of the court to the passer line.

5. The passer moves over to the shooter line.

Variations

Make it easier:

Make the passer line start closer in and just pass instead of dribble and pass.

Make it more difficult:

- Change the shooter line to the opposite side of the court.
- Make the shooter jump stop on the block and then shoot.
- Make the shooter shoot from a wing or guard position (use a spot marker for this shot).

Adaptations

- Lower the basket for players in wheelchairs.
- You can act as the passer.

Teaching Notes

- You will need to constantly remind the passer to make a leading pass.
- This is also a good fitness drill when the players become more skilled.

═══ ONE-BASE TEE BALL ═══

Players

Any size group

Area

Gym or outdoor open area

Skills

Hand–eye coordination • sequencing • turn taking

Equipment

Large plastic bat • Wiffle ball • tee or large cone • base

Activity

1. Set the Wiffle ball on the tee or cone.
2. One student at a time comes up to the tee as the batter.
3. The batter hits the ball off the tee, runs to retrieve the ball, and then tags the base, which is set up approximately 15 to 20 feet from the tee.
4. Encourage the player to continue running back to the tee and place the ball on top.
5. When a batter returns, he or she goes to the back of the line and the next batter steps up to the tee.
6. Allow as many at-bats as possible.
7. When using this game with higher-functioning students, allow other players to retrieve balls in the field.

Variations

Make it easier:

Use a larger and more brightly colored ball.

Make it more difficult:

⊙ Allow students to hit a pitched ball.
⊙ Eventually add more bases.
⊙ Play this game as a kickball game.

Adaptations

- ⊙ Assist students who find sequencing the tasks difficult.
- ⊙ Assist students in wheelchairs and students who are blind or visually impaired.
- ⊙ Use a bell ball for students who are blind or visually impaired.

Teaching Notes

- ⊙ This game is recommended for younger or lower-functioning individuals. It is a good game to help students start sequencing tasks and following directions in order to move on to more involved games.
- ⊙ They feel as if they hit a home run each time at bat.
- ⊙ Ultimately, this game can lead to participation in softball and baseball for many students, in a school setting or community league.

===ONE-ON-ONE BASKETBALL===

Players

Small or large group

Area

Basketball court

Skills

Defensive skills • offensive skills • transition

Equipment

Basketball

Activity

1. Arrange the players in two lines, one offense and one defense.
   The defensive line should be under the basket behind the end

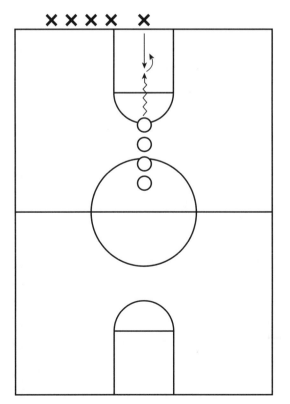

    boundary line, and the offensive line should be behind the arc above the free-throw line.

2. The ball starts in the defensive line. The defensive player rolls the ball to the offensive player and runs out to play defense.

3. The offensive player tries to take a shot.

4. If the defensive player gets the rebound after the shot, the defensive player then becomes the offense and play continues. You will need to help players remember their roles.

5. When play is over, the two switch lines.

6. This drill teaches the defensive player to keep his or her back to the basket and to stay between the basket and the offensive player at all times.

7. Also, this drill teaches the defensive player to keep his or her hands up in the air when the offensive player stops dribbling and attempts to shoot.

8. You must continually remind the defensive player of these rules.

Variations

Make it easier:

    Play can stop after the offensive player takes a shot until the group understands the transition from offense to defense.

Make it more difficult:

    Play continues until someone scores.

Adaptations

You can participate in the drill as an extra player for the offense to pass the ball to if in need of help.

Teaching Notes

◎ This drill is great for teaching defensive principles and strengthening one-on-one skills; zone play also becomes more aggressive.

◎ The players on defense learn to move instead of standing still.

◎ This drill also develops rebounding and shooting skills.

◎ The participants really enjoy this drill.

---ONE-ON-ONE SOCCER---

Players

Any size group

Area

Gym, outdoor open area, or soccer field

Skills

Dribbling under defensive pressure • passing • shooting • defense

Equipment

2 cones • soccer ball or gator-skin ball

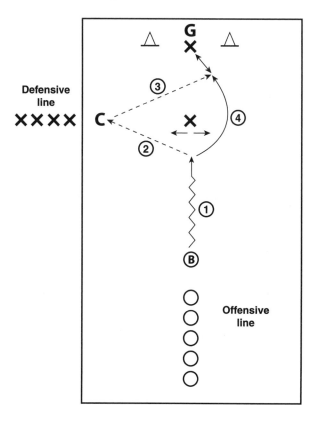

Activity

1. Set up the goal area with the cones. Arrange the players in two lines, an offense and a defense.
2. The first defensive player steps out on the playing area about 5 yards from the incoming dribbling offensive player.
3. The offensive player tries to evade the defensive player and take a shot against the goalie.
4. The offensive player may pass to you and then attempt to get open for a shot at the goalie.
5. If the defense obtains the ball from the offense, then play is over and the players switch lines.
6. The next two players would then start play.

Variations

Make it easier:

- ◎ Do not use a goalie.
- ◎ Make the playing area larger.
- ◎ Make the goal area larger.

Make it more difficult:

Make the goal area smaller.

Adaptations

Allow students in wheelchairs to start with the ball in their laps and then throw the ball to attempt a shot at the goal.

Teaching Notes

- ◎ This is a great drill.
- ◎ It takes one-on-one play a step further by adding you as a second offensive player.
- ◎ The offensive players also learn to move and get open to receive the ball before taking a shot.

═══ PADDLE BALL ═══

Players

4 to 15

Area

Gym or open area

Skills

Hand–eye coordination • tracking • teamwork

Equipment

Paddle • 12 or more Wiffle balls • crate or basket

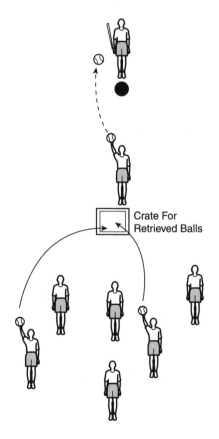

Crate For
Retrieved Balls

Activity

1. There is no particular setup for this activity.
2. One student at a time will attempt to hit balls thrown by you.
3. All other students will be scattered about the open area behind you for safety reasons. These students will retrieve hit balls and place them in a crate or basket.
4. The objective of retrieval is to see how many balls can be placed in the basket before the hitter is finished.
5. Continue play until all players take a turn at hitting.

Variations

Make it easier:

◎ If you focus on counting the balls in the basket, inform the students that they may throw balls to players closer to the basket.
◎ Move closer to the students, depending on skill level.
◎ Bounce the ball to hitters who track the ball better off a bounce.
◎ Roll the ball to hitters having a hard time tracking the ball.

Make it more difficult:

Move farther away from students, depending on skill level.

Adaptations

◎ Use hand over hand when needed.
◎ Tether the balls for students who are blind or visually impaired, or use a tee.

Teaching Notes

◎ This activity provides plenty of repetition and encourages students to work with others when retrieving.
◎ Elementary students enjoy this activity without counting the balls retrieved before the hitter is finished.
◎ This activity is also good for using up extra energy.
◎ Use for a skill day for middle or high school students and young adults.
◎ This game could ultimately lead to skill at table tennis.

--- PARTNER REBOUND ---

Players

Small or large group

Area

Basketball court

Skills

Rebounding • one-on-one skills

Equipment

Basketball

Activity

1. This is an advanced rebounding drill in which two players compete for a rebound.
2. The players each start on one side of the free-throw lane (at the elbow).
3. You shoot or toss the ball at the net, and the players attempt to rebound the ball.
4. The player successful at rebounding becomes the offense, and the other player becomes the defense.
5. The players are now in a one-on-one situation and continue to play until a basket is scored.

Variations

Make it easier:

◎ Stop play after the first shot.
◎ Do not use the one-on-one situation if the players do not understand offense and defense at this point.

Make it more difficult:

Add two defensive players who will also compete for the rebound.

Adaptations

◉ Move the players' starting point closer to the basket.

◉ Toss the ball up above students in wheelchairs.

Teaching Notes

The players learn to rebound more aggressively with this drill, and the drill allows the opportunity to teach one-on-one skills.

=== PICKUP DRIBBLE ===

Players

Small or large group

Area

Basketball court

Skills

Gaining control in a loose-ball situation • dribbling • shooting

Equipment

Basketballs

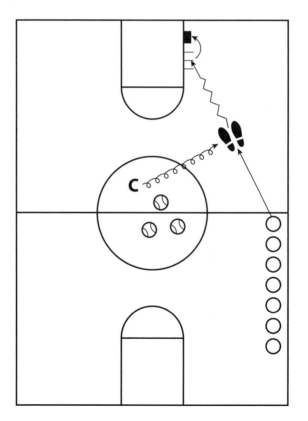

Activity

1. Instruct all players to line up along the right boundary line, starting at half-court. You will stand in the center circle with several basketballs.

2. As you give the "go" signal, roll the ball forward. The first person in line will chase the ball in an attempt to get control of the loose ball.

3. Instruct players to jump stop when gaining control of the ball before dribbling in for a layup shot.

4. Each player gets his or her own rebound, then runs back on the opposite side of the court and places the ball in the circle before returning to the line.

Variations

Make it easier:

Shorten the distance of the roll.

Make it more difficult:

⊚ Use different shots.

⊚ Add another player as a defender or a competitor after the ball.

Adaptations

Help players in wheelchairs or lower the basket.

Teaching Notes

⊚ This has been a very beneficial drill for my Special Olympics team.

⊚ The drill teaches the players to get control of the ball instead of trying to dribble through chaos.

⊚ It also reinforces dribbling and shooting skills.

=== PIN KICKBALL ===

Players

Small group

Area

Gym or open area

Skills

Kicking • sequencing • following rules

Equipment

6 to 12 bowling pins • playground ball or gator-skin ball for each player • spot markers

Activity

1. Line up the bowling pins, about 2 to 3 feet apart.
2. Form a parallel line approximately 15 feet across from the pins with spot markers.
3. Have each student stand on a spot marker with a ball.
4. When you give the "go" signal, each student kicks his or her ball from the line, attempting to knock the pins down.
5. After kicking, each student retrieves his or her ball and returns to the line. Students continue to kick until all pins are down.

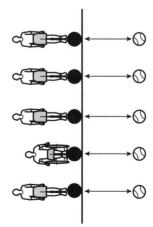

6. When all pins are down, celebrate and start over.

7. Use spot markers for the pins, and allow the students to reset the game.

Variations

Make it easier:

Shorten the distance between the line and the pins.

Make it more difficult:

Lengthen the distance between the lines.

Adaptations

⊚ Use a ramp for students in wheelchairs, and allow them to roll the ball at the pins.

⊚ Use a tethered ball for students who are blind or visually impaired, and allow them to roll the ball if necessary.

Teaching Notes

⊚ This game is appropriate for younger or lower-functioning students. It is a good activity to practice kicking a stationary ball and is a good lead-up activity for kickball or kicking a rolling ball.

⊚ When using this game with lower-functioning students, you may need to retrieve the balls for the kicker or assign a peer helper.

⊚ Reinforce that this is a team activity.

⊚ This game and others that emphasize the same skills can ultimately prepare students to participate in a soccer game, within a school environment or community league.

=== POWER PULL ===

Players

Any size group

Area

Open area

Skills

Strengthening

Equipment

Rope • 2 spot markers • gloves

Activity

1. This is basically a one-on-one tug of war game.
2. Place two spot markers approximately 10 feet apart.
3. Tie a loop in the rope on both ends for the players to hold on to.
4. A belay rope is perfect to use; however, any nylon rope 1 to 2 inches in diameter will work.
5. Provide gloves for the players to protect against rope burn.
6. Each player will start with one foot on a spot marker.
7. When you give the "go" signal, the players start pulling in an attempt to pull the opposing player's foot off the spot marker.
8. When one of the players steps off the spot marker, give the "stop" signal.
9. Two new players then take a turn.

Variations

Make it easier:

- ☉ As a safety precaution, you may choose to stand in the middle and hold the rope to take up the slack if someone lets go.
- ☉ Use boundary lines instead of spot markers.

Make it more difficult:

Designate the right or left arm for pulling for advanced players; this could be a problem for students with low upper body strength.

Adaptations

- ⊙ Definitely hold the rope for less skilled players.
- ⊙ Allow students in wheelchairs to sit on the spot marker. Choose a smaller, less skilled player as the opponent.

Teaching Notes

This is a great activity for teaching students to use all of their strength. They often do not understand this concept.

--- REBOUND AND SCORE ---

Players

Small or large group

Area

Basketball court

Skills

Rebounding • shooting

Equipment

Basketballs

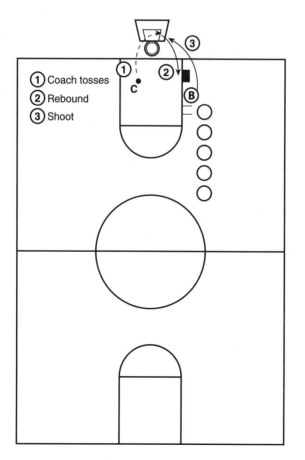

1 Coach tosses
2 Rebound
3 Shoot

Activity

1. Stand on one side of the basket on the block (the black box on each side of the free-throw lane closest to the basket); the player stands on the other side of the basket on the block.
2. Toss the ball over the net (using the backboard if possible). The player jumps to rebound the ball and then shoots it.
3. Have several balls on hand so that you can continue tossing balls for the rebounding player.
4. New players rotate into rebounding position after four or five rebounds.

Variations

Make it easier:

Use the same adaptations below for less skilled players.

Make it more difficult:

You can act as a defensive player against the shooter.

Adaptations

⊙ Toss the ball above the head of the rebounding player instead of over the net.

⊙ Hold the ball above the head of the rebounding player, and allow the player to rebound without a toss.

Teaching Notes

The players need to be reminded often to jump for the rebound, but their timing does improve with this drill.

━━ ROLLOUT DRIBBLE ━━

Players

Any size group

Area

Gym, outdoor open area, or soccer field

Skills

Chasing loose balls • getting control of the ball • dribbling

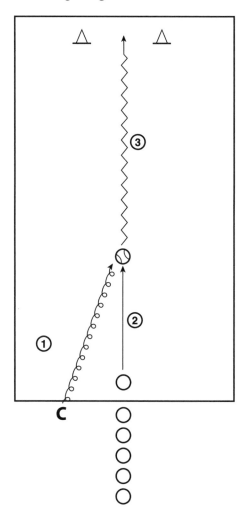

Equipment

Soccer balls or gator-skin balls

Activity

1. This drill will teach players to "hustle" for the ball. The players all start in the same line on one end of the field. Only one player at a time participates in the drill.
2. You will roll the ball forward far enough ahead of the player so that he or she needs to run or sprint to catch up with the loose ball.
3. The player then dribbles to the end of the field and back down the sideline to return the ball to you.
4. Start with five or more balls to keep the players moving. This is a great fitness drill.

Variations

Make it easier:

Roll the ball closer to the players.

Make it more difficult:

- ◎ Add a goal and even a goalie once the players become skilled in their dribbling.
- ◎ Allow two players to chase after one ball.

Adaptations

Adjust the speed of the rolled ball according to skill levels.

Teaching Notes

- ◎ This drill helped my players comprehend the importance of hustling for the ball.
- ◎ They started to play harder after this drill.

▀▀▀ SOCCER TAG ▀▀▀

Players

Small or large group

Area

Gym, outdoor open area, or soccer field

Skills

Dribbling • shooting • fitness

Equipment

4 cones for boundaries • 1 or more softer soccer balls

Activity

1. Set up a playing area about the size of half a basketball court for small groups and about the size of the whole court for large groups.
2. Choose one or two players to be "it." All other players should be scattered about the playing area.
3. The "it" player or players will dribble about the area, trying to tag other fleeing players on the foot with the soccer ball.
4. Instruct and demonstrate that the "it" players must kick the ball on the ground when attempting to tag other players.
5. When a player is tagged or steps out of bounds, he or she must run around the playing field before returning to play.

Variations

Make it easier:

Use more players as "its."

Make it more difficult:

Use a predetermined exercise instead of running around the playing area.

Adaptations

- ◎ Shadow less skilled dribblers, and help them with ball control.
- ◎ Push students in wheelchairs if they are not mobile. Attach a hockey stick to the chair for controlling the ball, or allow these students to roll the ball at other players.
- ◎ Lead students who are blind or visually impaired with a tether, and assist with ball control.

Teaching Notes

Because of coordination and skill levels, this game is not a hazard, or does not get out of control for the players.

Players

Small or large group

Area

Gym, multipurpose room, or outdoor open area

Skills

Dribbling • shooting • passing if desired

Equipment

2 cones for each goal • 4 to 6 bowling pins for each goal • soccer balls or indoor soccer balls • spot markers

Activity

1. Set up the goal area, approximately 12 feet wide, and place the bowling pins between the cones. Use a spot marker or cone to

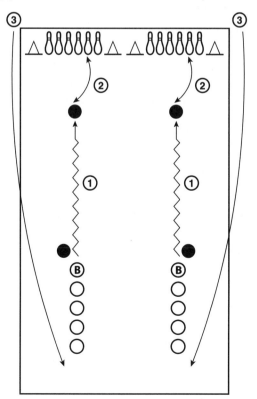

signify the beginning of the line for dribbling and a spot marker to signify the shooting area.

2. All students will start in the line and take turns dribbling the ball to the shooting area to take a shot at the goal.

3. Inform the group that this is a team effort to knock all the pins down.

4. Allow the group to do this several times, resetting each time all pins are knocked down.

5. Set up as many goals as needed for the group size.

6. Use a timer to motivate students if needed.

Variations

Make it easier:

Adjust the distance from the kicking spot to the goal.

Make it more difficult:

- Add another line, and designate one line to dribble and pass and the other line to receive and shoot.
- Use a goalie to protect the pins.

Adaptations

- Use attachments on wheelchairs for the players to push the ball, such as a box on the front of the chairs or a hockey stick attached to the side.
- Assist players in wheelchairs and students who are blind or visually impaired.

Teaching Notes

- You will need to teach the dribbling player to pass the ball in front of the receiving player when adding the dribble and pass line. You will also need to give verbal prompts for this skill.
- The pins motivate the players to make controlled, accurate kicks. Sometimes I set this drill up as a game with two parallel lines approximately 15 feet long. The students are divided equally into two teams, and the objective of the game is to kick the ball in an attempt to knock down the other team's pins. Use lots of soft balls for this game version.

--- VOLLEY TOSS ---

Players

Small group

Area

Gym or open area

Skills

Underhand tossing • catching

Equipment

Volleyball net • 8-1/2-inch gator-skin ball • 4 cones or spot markers for boundaries

Activity

1. Set up the volleyball net.
2. Use cones or spot markers for side and end boundaries.
3. Divide students into two teams, one on each side of the net.
4. Organize students into two rows.
5. Play starts by one team tossing underhand over the net to the other team.
6. The receiving team tries to catch the ball in the air or after one bounce.
7. If the receiving team catches the ball, play continues; the player who caught the ball throws it back over the net.
8. If the receiving team does not catch the ball, a point is awarded to the throwing team.

Variations

Make it easier:

For smaller groups, adjust boundaries to make a smaller playing area.

Make it more difficult:

Allow no bounces for more skilled players.

Adaptations

- You or a peer helper can catch the ball for any students having difficulty; the students can then toss the ball back over themselves.
- Lower or raise the net according to ability levels.

Teaching Notes

- This is basically a game of throwing and catching, but it teaches the students to stay focused.
- The score does not seem to matter to the players; they are mostly focused on catching the ball.
- Sometimes as a closing activity, I use a beach ball and allow the students to volley the ball as in volleyball.
- Ultimately, this game could lead to games of traditional volleyball for your students.

REFERENCES AND SUGGESTED READINGS

Bryant, R. and E. Oliver. 1974. *Complete elementary physical education guide*. West Nyack, NY: Parker.

Clumpner, R. 2003. *Sport progressions*. Champaign, IL: Human Kinetics.

Halliday, N. 1999. Developing self-esteem through challenge education experiences. *JOPERD* 70 (6): 51-66.

Henderson, K., M. Glancy, and S. Little. 1999. Putting the fun into physical activity. *JOPERD* 70 (2): 43-49.

Hughes, F. 1995. *Children, play, and development*. Boston: Allyn & Bacon.

Kasser, S. 1995. *Inclusive games: Movement fun for everyone*. Champaign, IL: Human Kinetics.

Nichols, B. 1994. *Moving and learning: The elementary school physical education experience*. St. Louis: Mosby.

Project Adventure Inc. Workshop. 1995-2004. Author's notes from seminars. Covington, GA.

Rohnke, C. 1989. *Cowstails and cobras II: A guide to games, initiatives, ropes courses, and adventure curriculum*. Dubuque, IA: Kendall/Hunt.

Sherrill, C. 1998. *Adapted physical activity, recreation and sport: Cross-disciplinary and lifespan*. Boston: McGraw-Hill.

ABOUT THE AUTHOR

Pattie Rouse has more than 20 years of experience teaching physical education to persons with disabilities. Building on her tremendous success using games to help all groups of learners develop team-building skills, she has also trained other teachers to use the same type of team-building programs. This book is an outgrowth of the positive results her methods have engendered.

Rouse currently works for Georgia's Cherokee County school system, where she teaches adapted physical education at 11 schools. She is also co-coordinator and coach for the Cherokee County Special Olympics. She holds a BSED in health and physical education from Georgia Southern University and a master's of education in integrated studies from Cambridge College in Boston. She also has been trained in instructional strategies for children with emotional and behavioral disabilities, adventure-based counseling, and developmental therapy for children with autism. In 1995, Rouse received the Teacher of the Year award from Sixes Elementary School. Rouse lives in Marietta, Georgia, with her five dogs and cat. In her spare time, she enjoys hiking, biking, reading, and volunteering with dog rescue groups.

*You'll find
other outstanding
games resources at*

www.HumanKinetics.com